Prized Quilts

The Omaha World-Herald Quilt Contests

By Donna di Natale

It's Time to Get Ready
Middle West Women
Prize Contest
Evening Showing
of Quilt Exhibit
Into This Quilt

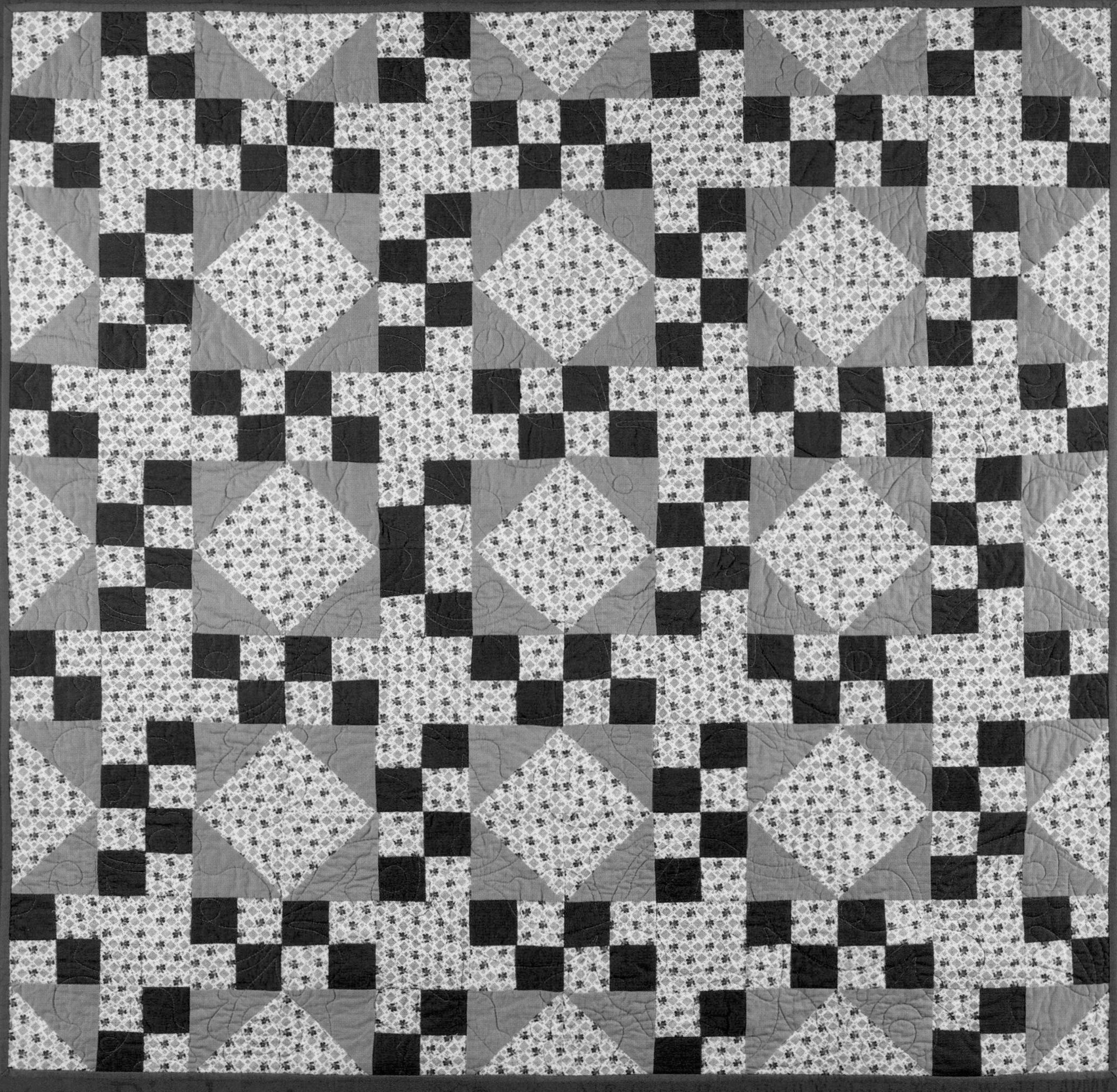

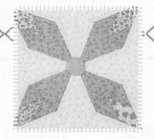

Prized Quilts

The Omaha World-Herald Quilt Contests

By Donna di Natale
Editor: Kent Richards
Designer: Kelly Ludwig
Photography: Aaron T. Leimkuehler
Illustration: Lon Eric Craven
Technical Editor: Jane Miller
Photo Editor: Jo Ann Groves
Published by:
Kansas City Star Books
1729 Grand Blvd.
Kansas City, Missouri, USA 64108
All rights reserved

First edition, first printing
ISBN - 978-1-61169-104-7
Library of Congress Control Number: 2013946078

Printed in the United States of America by Walsworth Publishing Co., Marceline, MO
To order copies, call StarInfo at (816) 234-4473.

PickleDish.com
The Quilter's Home Page

KANSAS CITY STAR
QUILTS
Continuing the Tradition

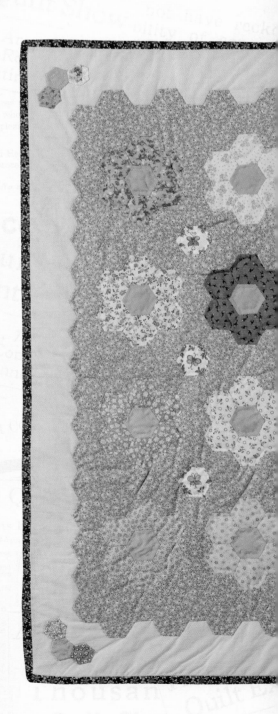

Table of Contents

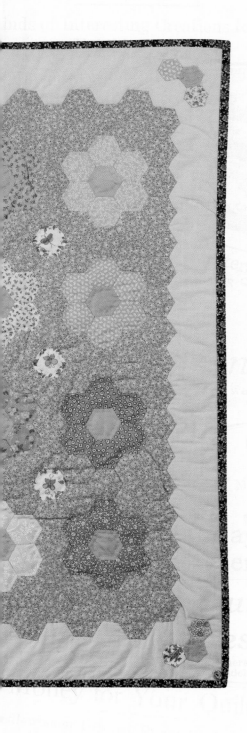

Acknowledgements

Thank you, Doug Weaver, for recognizing that the Omaha World-Herald quilt contests were worthy of a story, and for trusting my ability to tell the story. Indeed there is a story to be told, one that reaches far beyond what I've been able to share here.

Sincere thanks to Jan Stehlik for sharing her research of the Omaha World-Herald quilt contest with me. Her research paper "Quilt Patterns and Contests of the Omaha World-Herald, 1921-1941" (*Uncoverings*, Laurel Horton, Editor, American Quilt Study Group, 1990) was invaluable in gathering information about the contests. I'm happy to say I was able to uncover more information to add to her extensive notes.

It may seem trite to say that without certain people, this book would never have seen the light of day. But in this case, it is true. Faced with drafting patterns and making 10 quilts in 10 months, in addition to writing the text, I was pleased when friends stepped forward to help. Thank you to Marilyn Carr for making the Blue Star Turned to Gold and the Star Baby quilt. Thank you Susan Thorup for the use of your Butterfly quilt and Patches Tumbler quilt. Thank you to Janette Sheldon for your amazing paper piecing of the Spinning Pinwheel. Thank you to machine quilters Freda Smith, Donna Simpson, Janiece Cline, David Hurd and Lindsay Lawing for bringing life to the pieced and appliquéd tops.

Many thanks to my team at Kansas City Star Quilts:

▷ To Kent Richards, my editor, I appreciate your patience when it took me so long to finish this book. It was a pleasure to work with you.

▷ To my designer, Kelly Ludwig, who understood my vision for this book even when I had a difficult time explaining it. Your design made this book come alive. You totally rock!

▷ To Jane Miller for catching my errors, especially on the Antique Basket Doll Quilt. My head is still reeling.

▷ To Eric Craven for turning my scribbles into art. I really appreciate your skill.

▷ To Edie McGinnis for advice and support, and for her unique ability to create just the right setting for the photographs.

▷ To Aaron Leimkuehler for your photographic skill and for understanding what I wanted to accomplish.

▷ To Jo Ann Groves for working her magic on the photographs. I don't understand exactly what you do, which is why I call it magic.

Thank you to my husband, Patrick, for your support, advice, drafting and photography skills, a shoulder to cry on, an ear to bend and most of all, your patience. I still promise to clean up my sewing room one of these days.

And a final thanks to Murphy, my very special spotted Tabby cat and quality control manager. No quilt is finished until it has Murphy's approval.

"The best place on earth for taking a nap is on a quilt." - Murphy

Shawnee Town 1929 Museum

A special thank you to Charlie Pautler, Museum Director, and to the staff and volunteers at the Shawnee Town 1929 Museum, where we photographed the projects in this book. The museum farmstead, shops, Town Hall and other buildings allow visitors to experience a typical day in and around the farm community of Shawnee, Kansas, in the late 1920s. Its authentic collections, exhibits and events provide hands-on experiences for people of all ages.

The museum was a perfect setting to depict life in the Midwest of the 1920s. Shannon Hsu took time from her busy schedule as Curator of Collections to assist with the settings and explain the role and importance of the home's artifacts in day-to-day life. While indoor plumbing and electricity were common in cities, the pump by the kitchen sink, the icebox in the corner and the oil lamps on the walls were the standard for rural homes. When visiting the home, it's easy to picture women tracing templates onto feed sack fabric and sewing pieces together on the treadle sewing machine. No wonder they were so proud of their accomplishments.

The Museum is located at 11501 West 57th Street, Shawnee, Kansas 66203. For hours and additional information go to www.shawneetown.org or call 913-248-2360.

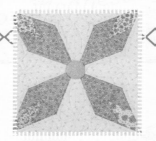

Introduction

The Omaha World-Herald bldg. in 1942

As I began writing this book in the summer of 2012, I was reminded of the summers that people lived through back in the 30s: daily temperatures of more than 100 degrees, fields empty of crops, dust blown up against doors, and no air conditioning or place to go to avoid the heat. Yet women, children, and men all over the state of Nebraska, the surrounding states, and as far away as Hawaii, stitched pieces of fabric together to create quilts worthy of ribbons and prizes. Not just a few quilts, hundreds of quilts were entered each year in contests sponsored by the Omaha (Nebraska) World-Herald newspaper. And thousands of people viewed the quilts in department stores such as Brandeis, Kilpatrick's, and Sears, Roebuck and Company.

What was it that compelled these people to display their handwork and compete for prizes? Pride? Competition? Money? As Carolyn McCormick so rightly put it in the title of her book, *Hard Times, Splendid Quilts*, these people were faced with everyday hardships, regardless of their standard of living. Yet they found the resources to create things of beauty — one bright object that commanded pride and respect over all else.

Beginning in the late 1920s, many newspapers and magazines published quilt block patterns in their home arts or women's section to attract readership. Patterns were printed individually and in series.

In Omaha, Nebraska, the local newspaper, the World-Herald, enthusiastically joined the quilting revival. Quilt patterns were printed weekly, and sometimes twice a week — midweek and again Sunday. To give you some idea of the effect this had on Midwestern families, more than 121,000 copies of the World-Herald were distributed every Sunday morning. Huge presses, capable of printing 50,000 complete Sunday papers per hour, rolled out papers on conveyer belts, where they were stamped and bundled for delivery. Forty-five thousand copies were delivered in Omaha alone. The remaining 76,000 papers were shipped by truck to towns in Nebraska and surrounding states, where that week's quilt pattern was anticipated by numerous men and women.

In 1931, the World-Herald took quilting patterns in the newspaper one step further by sponsoring a quilt contest that would become an annual event for the next 10 years. Local department and home furnishings stores joined in the effort as both co-sponsors and exhibition halls. In 1939, the contest entries were exhibited on the 10th floor of the Brandeis store — 10 floors! One wonders what fabulous merchandise filled all those floors on a daily basis. I'm sure the department stores saw their participation as a way of drawing people into the store and attracting new business from viewers who came by the thousands.

Entries

There was never a fee to enter a quilt in the contest, and there was never an admission fee charged to view the exhibit. Even at times when the store was only open for the exhibit and no merchandise was sold, admission was entirely free to everyone. Certainly the number of viewers was influenced by this fact, as well as the desire to see the beautiful handcrafted quilts.

Entry blanks were printed in the newspaper, and those wishing to enter a quilt were instructed to fill out the blank and send it to the paper as soon as possible. The entry blanks were not actual entry forms. They were intended simply to give the sponsors and judges some idea of the number of entries they could expect.

When quilts were mailed or delivered to the host store, one very strict rule applied. The entrant or owner was instructed to have their name stitched on a label attached to the back of their quilt for identification. I wonder how many of those quilts still have that label on the back.

Judges

There were typically two, and sometimes three, judges each year. The judge's names were usually withheld until after the show opened and in some years were never announced. Seldom was there any explanation as to the judges' expertise or qualifications as a judge. Two frequent judges, Mrs. A. D. Peter and Mrs. C. C. Belden, were listed as "connoisseurs" of quilts. Others who served as judges: Mrs. R. Kulakofsky, Mrs. Sidney Smith, Mrs. M. T. White, Mrs. A. M. Smith, Mrs. Edith Louise Wagoner (weaving instructor at the Omaha Social Settlement), Elizabeth Ryner, and

Gwenndolyn Beeler (home economics instructor at Omaha University). Nadine Bradley, director of the World-Herald's women's department in 1938, served as one of three judges that year.

Where are these quilts now?

Little information could be found about the winning entries, and what information could be uncovered revealed only names and addresses. No photographs of the winning quilts ever appeared in print.

I first became aware of these contests when working on my first book, *Anna's Quilt*. Anna was my Aunt Anna, my father's oldest sister. In 1938, Anna entered her floral bouquet quilt in the World-Herald contest and won a blue ribbon in her division. The ribbon is still attached to the back of the quilt and remains a part of the quilt's story to this day.

This book was written to pay homage to the people who entered their quilts in the contests, and to the World-Herald and the department stores that displayed the quilts. While the contests may have started as a means to attract business, what they actually accomplished cannot be measured in dollars and cents. Rather, the contests provided an opportunity for quilters to display their skills and compete for valuable prizes that in turn made life better in difficult times.

So come along, and join me in this journey as we uncover the quilt contests of the World-Herald in the 1930s.

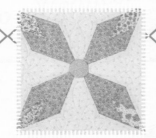

Winner's Circle

Contest winners were announced each year toward the end of the show. The winner's name and address was given, along with the category and prize won. However, photographs of the winning quilts were never printed.

Even without photographs, I felt it was important to include the names and city of residence of the winning entrants in this book. It is my sincere hope that someone will read this list and discover the name of a family member or friend. Perhaps this list will reveal unknown information about a quilt that you own. So much about quilts has been lost over the years. Even the tiniest bit of information can add so much to our treasured quilts.

This list includes all of the winners by year. One person, Mrs. L. L. Berthe of North Platte, won 1st place in four different years, twice with the same Bowl of Flowers quilt. Two adult males won prizes: Arthur Cahay of Omaha, in 1935, and Arden Berquist of Omaha, in 1939. Both won for Unique Quilts. In 1937, Mrs. John M. Hornish won in two categories: Antique Quilts and General Pieced Quilts.

If you recognize a name, or know of a winning quilt, please contact me at ddinatale@kcstar.com. I'd love to print an addendum to this book with more information on the quilts, quilt makers and the families who continue to care for the quilts. When I discovered that my aunt had won a prize in 1938, I was surprised to learn that not only did the family still own the quilt, but they still had the wing back chair that she had won. My aunt's quilt is now a part of the collection at the International Quilt Study Center Museum in Lincoln, Nebraska - a fitting place for a prized quilt.

How to Read This List:

—Year—

Co-sponsor/host store

Date the winners were announced
Headline
First line on announcement
The winners are listed in order of 1st, 2nd and 3rd. Their state of residence is Nebraska unless otherwise noted.

—1931—

Brandeis Store

June 12, 1931
Skill with Needle Wins

For skill in the ancient craft of needlework, as demonstrated by the beautiful quilts displayed in the World-Herald show last week, 21 prizes were announced today.

Best Farm Life quilt made by woman over 65 years old

Mrs. Nat Childs, Omaha
Mrs. Elizabeth Chapin, Omaha
Mrs. Jennie McGoven, Omaha

Best Farm Life quilt made by a child under 14 years

Louise Logeman, Bennington
Ernest Bratetic, Omaha
R. W. Reynolds, Omaha

Best Farm Life quilt made by a single woman

Phyllis Kapella, Omaha

Note: The category of Farm life quilts made by single women was poorly subscribed. The 2nd and 3rd place prizes were awarded as additional prizes in the Unique and Antique quilt categories.

Best Farm Life quilt made by a married woman

Mrs. D. E. Jackson, Paxton
Mrs. Lillian Hartwell, Omaha
Mrs. Anna Franks, Omaha

Best Antique quilt

Mrs. W. B. Kinsie, Omaha
Mrs. C. W. Baker, Omaha
Mrs. Jo Grattan, Stanton

Best Unique quilt

Mrs. Guy Zielger, Ashland
Mrs. Ione Gilliam, Council Bluffs, Iowa
Mrs. Ray McMaken, Plattsmouth
Mrs. H. D. Miller, Omaha

Best quilt made from previous blocks printed in the World-Herald

Mrs. A. E. Perley, Omaha
Miss Grata Sass, Omaha (Benson)
Mrs. E. L. Livingston, Omaha
Mrs. Catherina Stenius, Omaha

—1932—

Kilpatrick's Store

October 26, 1932
Prize Quilts on Display During Rest of Week

To reward skill in the ancient art of needlework, as shown in the display of quilts in the World-Herald quilt exhibition last week, 21 prizes were announced Monday. The judges examined 730 quilts, viewed by more than 30 thousand people last week at the Kilpatrick store.

State Flower quilts made by women over 65

Mrs. Jennie Tulburt, Omaha
Mrs. M. J. Lynch, Omaha
Mrs. William Siekkotter, Gretna

State Flower quilts made by children under 14

Marie Marchiselli, Omaha
(Only one prize was awarded.)

State Flower quilts made by unmarried women

Bertha Anderson, Dunbar
Phyllis Kapella, Omaha
Cecilia Schultz, Council Bluffs, Iowa

State Flower quilt made by married women

Mrs. HJ. G. Schmidt, Omaha
Mrs. A. Kimler, Omaha
Mrs. R. S. Childs, Omaha

Antique quilts

Mrs. Josephine Mygatt, Omaha
Mrs. A. L. Nielson, Harlan, Iowa
Miss Mary P. Doyle, Omaha

Unique quilts

Mrs. L. L. Berthe, Torrington, Wyoming
Mrs. Louis Gatzemeyer, Bancroft
Mrs. Mary Gill, Omaha

Quilts made from blocks previously printed in the World-Herald

Mrs. Albina Walasek, Omaha
Mrs. Ernest Farrington, Chadron
Mrs. Mary Haworth, Elwood

—1933—

Sears, Roebuck and Company
September 10, 1933
Two Omaha Women Are Among those Capturing First Place
The judges said they found the awarding a difficult but pleasant task and awards in most divisions were made for the fineness and exquisiteness of the ancient craft of needlework.

Fruit Basket quilt made by women over 60
Martha H. Graves, York
Mrs. R. Larsen, Omaha
(No 3rd place was announced)

Fruit Basket quilt made by married or single woman
Margaret Werner, Humphrey
Mrs. Susie Childs, Omaha
Mrs. Joe Andrea, Rockport, Missouri

Best Unique quilt
Mrs. L. L. Berthe, North Platte
Mrs. Lloyd Arnold, Omaha
Mrs. J. Z. Roberts, Brownville

Best Antique quilt
Mrs. C. W. Baker, Omaha
Mrs. Ed Oekke, Nebraska City
Mrs. Maude Walker, Council Bluffs, Iowa

Quilts made from blocks previously printed in the World-Herald
Mrs. Sarah Crowell, Omaha
Augusta Kimbler, Omaha
Mrs. J. E. Gray, Omaha

—1934—

Union Outfitting Company
September 16, 1934
Thousands at Exhibit; Still on Display at Union Outfitting
Climaxing a week's inspection of the finest quilts in the middle-west, which have attracted thousands of people during the past week, is the announcement of winners by judges of the World-Herald's fourth annual quilt contest.

Three Little Pigs quilt made by women over 60
Mrs. Kate Hainey, Fremont
Mrs. W. Hall, Pierce
Mrs. Nick Mueller, Fremont

Three Little Pigs quilts made by women 17 to 59 year of age
Mrs. Henry J. Bohney, Council Bluffs, Iowa
Mrs. Betty Trout, North Platte
Mrs. Edwin Lewis, Omaha

Quilts made by children under 16 years
Bernice Vanderheiden, Randolph
Stuart Barlow, Kearney
Virginia Hollis, Omaha

General open division
Mrs. A. M. Carey, Council Bluffs, Iowa
Mrs. Emma Conrey, Omaha
Belle M. Herrick, Omaha

Antique quilts
Mrs. I. C. Revell, Shenandoah, Iowa
Mrs. Bruce P. Caywood, Hastings
Mrs. W. Merrill, Council Bluffs, Iowa

Unique quilts
Mrs. L. E. August, Palmyra
Mrs. G. B. Scot, Omaha
Mrs. Vivian Oblinger, Omaha

Quilts made from blocks previously printed in the World-Herald
Mrs. Mark Woodward, Omaha
Mrs. T. L. Yard, Omaha
Mrs. H. Von Seggern, Hooper

—1935—

5 Thousand
at Quilt Show

Prizes Are Awarded;
Sears, Roebuck Store
to Continue Display

Sears, Roebuck and Company

September 7, 1935

5 Thousand at Quilt Show

More than five thousand persons strolled Friday night past the hundreds of quilts entered in the contest … It was the largest such show in Omaha history. Both attendance and entries surpassed previous marks.

Flower Basket quilts

Mrs. L. L. Berthe, North Platte
Mrs. Sarah Crowell, Omaha
Mrs. A. W. Boal, Council Bluffs, Iowa

Quilts made by children under 16 years

Helen Brueggeman, Omaha
Virginia Hollis, Omaha
Claire Greenfields, Omaha

General open division

Miss Mary Bostyn, Spalding
Mrs. M. S. Moore, Omaha
Mrs. Clara Carey, Council Bluffs, Iowa

Antique quilts

Mrs. George J. Viehmeyer, Stapleton
Mrs. W. C. Edmiston, Ralston
Laura Ament, Omaha

Unique quilts

Mrs. James Campin, Imogene, Iowa
Arthur Cahay, Omaha
Mrs. James Fisher, Mount Ayr, Iowa

Quilts made from blocks previously printed in the World-Herald

Mrs. B. P. Collins, Omaha
Mrs. T. L. Yards, Omaha
Mrs. E. Svoboda, Omaha

—1936—

Brandeis Store

September 20, 1936

Prize Quilts Are Selected

Eighteen of the Midwest's most outstanding quilts will be found on the sixth floor and seventh floor at the Brandeis store…the 18 quilt champions of the annual World-Herald contest and show.

Quilts made by children under 16 years

Betty Stone, Omaha
Betty Westerman, Omaha
Virginia Hollis, Omaha

General open, pieced quilts

Mrs. D. C. Nickell, Council Bluffs, Iowa
Mrs. Leonore O. Donaldson, Corning, Iowa
Mrs. Claus Ehlers, Scribner

General open, embroidered and appliquéd quilts

Maime Colter, Omaha
Mrs. Gussie Wheelock, Ravenna
Mrs. J. B. McGrew, Omaha

Antique quilts

Mrs. Fred B. Smith, Nebraska City
Mrs. Leonard Mygatt, Omaha
Mrs. W. Hann, Council Bluffs, Iowa

Unique quilts

Mrs. L. E. August, Palmyra
Mrs. G. B. Scott, Council Bluffs, Iowa
Mrs. James N. Lund, Blair

World-Herald pattern series quilts

Mrs. E. G. Shellenberger, Omaha
Mrs. G. Brownhill, Omaha
Mrs. Claudia Hamilton, Council Bluffs, Iowa

William Dorrance General Store,
Fairmont, Nebraska, ca. 1930.

Lots of Warmth in This Contest

Mrs. Audrey Wright, 3538 Avenue A, Council Bluffs, is shown here with a few of the quilt show entries which have been received in The World-Herald-Orchard & Wilhelm quilt show, September 12 to 17. Eighteen of the quilts in the contest will be chosen as winners and their owners will be awarded prizes including a two-piece living room davenport and chair set, a General Electric radio, several occasional chairs and a fitted sewing cabinet. Tuesday, September 6, has been set as entry deadline for entry of the quilts at Orchard & Wilhelm store.

—1937—

Hayden Brothers

September 26, 1937

Large Crowds View Annual Exhibit

After a week's study of more than three hundred quilts entered in the World-Herald's annual quilt contest, judges Saturday afternoon completed the task of selecting the first three bests in six divisions. … Except in one instance, the judges, who marked their own score cards privately, were unanimous in the selections.

Antique quilts

Mrs. I. D. Baker, Omaha
Mrs. A. Coyle, Omaha
Mrs. John M. Hornish, Omaha

Unique quilts

Mrs. G. B. Scott, Council Bluffs, Iowa
Mrs. W. G. James, Omaha
Mrs. H. F. McIntosh, Omaha

General appliqué and embroidered

Mrs. John Koubsky, Omaha
Mrs. D. W. Dudgeon, Omaha
Mrs. Oscar Shepard, Red Oak, Iowa

General pieced

Mrs. John M. Hornish, Omaha
Mrs. R. C. Hawkins, Butte
Mrs. Louis Schack, Harlan, Iowa

Quilts made by children

Roberta Welsh, Brule
Robert Bruce Dehl, Omaha
Mazie Maslowsky, Omaha

World-Herald pattern

Mrs. R. O. Haskins, Nebraska City
Mrs. Gertrude Spalta, Council Bluffs, Iowa
Mrs. Walter Duda, Omaha

—1938—

Orchard & Wilhelm

September 15, 1938

18 Persons Get Prizes in Quilt Show Contest

Four hundred dollars in merchandise will be divided among seven women from Omaha, three from Council Bluffs and eight from outstate Nebraska — winners of the World-Herald Orchard & Wilhelm 1938 quilt show.

Quilt makers under 16 years of age

Edna Weber, Omaha
Betty Stone, Omaha
Mrs. D. O. Kipling (entrant), Omaha

Antique quilts

Mrs. Bruce Caywood, Hastings
Mrs. John Buchanan, Omaha
Mrs. J. S. Coltan, Omaha

Unique quilts

Miss Anna Scott, Council Bluffs, Iowa
Miss Clara Jaquier, Council Bluffs, Iowa
Mrs. G. H. Boetel, Omaha

General open appliqué and embroidered

Mrs. W. F. Wenke, Pender
Agnes Hibeler, Millard
Mrs. R. Pytlik, Howells

General open pieced

Mrs. John Westcott, Comstock
Mrs. Fred Rapp, Council Bluffs, Iowa
Mrs. John Sleutvill, Omaha

Quilts made with World-Herald quilt block patterns

Mrs. Margaret Donitz, Elkhorn
Mrs. A. F. Almen, Mead
Mrs. M. A. Shepard, Nebraska City

—1939—

Brandeis Store

September 23, 1939
Many Prizes Are Awarded at Quilt Show
Valued at $415, the quilt show prizes were awarded by three Omaha judges, who were careful to weed from the list of winners persons who had won World-Herald sponsored quilt shows during the last three years.
Note: The only available article listing the winners was virtually unreadable. The author apologizes for any misspellings or omissions.

Quilts made by children under 16

Elaine Zahcek, Crete
W. D. Lyon, Omaha

General open pieced

Patty Peake, Council Bluffs, Iowa
Mrs. Edward Rohmeier, Humboldt
Mrs. W. D. Collette, Brady

General open appliqué and embroidered

Mrs. Arnold Luschen, Gretna
Mrs. A. M. Carey, Council Bluffs, Iowa
Mrs. Howard O. Graham, Omaha

Antique quilts

Miss Marian Uhe, David City
Mrs. L. Eissman, Omaha
Mrs. J. A. True, Council Bluffs, Iowa

Unique quilts

Mrs. Rene Huffman, Beaver Crossing
Mrs. L. O. Tilker, Omaha
Arden Berquist, Omaha

World-Herald quilt pattern quilts

Mrs. W. Alven, Omaha
Marie Freed, West Point
Mrs. A. W. Reid, Council Bluffs, Iowa

—1940—

Sears, Roebuck Company

October 3, 1940
Quilt Prizes Are Awarded
Winners in the World-Herald Sears, Roebuck quilt show were announced today. The winning quilts as well as seven hundred others, with a total value of 32 thousand dollars, will be on exhibit at Sears' second floor for the rest of the week. Wednesday, two thousand persons visited the show.

General open pieced quilts

Mrs. Anna Gerken, Concordia, Missouri
Mrs. Estella Ward, Red Oak, Iowa
Mrs. I. M. Albertson, Council Bluffs, Iowa
Honorable Mention
Mrs. G. D. Lyons, Omaha
Mary J. Stone, Omaha

General open appliqué and embroidered quilts

Mrs. J. A. Chagstrom, Omaha
Mrs. E. J. Hornberger, Omaha
Mrs. Homer Scheitel, Falls City
Honorable Mention
Mrs. H. Tolbert, Oakland, Iowa
Mrs. J. B. Brain, Omaha

Quilt Show Held Over Two Days
WORLD-HERALD QUILT SHOW
A Man Enters the Quilt Contest; Others Sought for Prize Division

Quilts made by children under 16

Miss Frances Kramer, West Point
Vada Brothers, La Platte
Roberta Welsh, Brule
Honorable Mention
Della Mae Uhe, David City
Doris Headley, Omaha
Leonard Zajicek, Crete

Antique quilts

Mrs. Ed Oelko, Nebraska City
Mrs. W. E. Branam, Omaha
Mrs. Isa D. Baker, Omaha
Honorable Mention
Mrs. Ray Bayne, Omaha
Mrs. Barbie Johnston, Omaha

Quilts made from World-Herald quilt blocks

Mrs. L. L. Berthe, North Platte
Mrs. H. C. Woodruff,
Omaha

Mrs. M. A. Shepard, Nebraska City
Honorable Mention
Mrs. E. A. Mischnik, Omaha
Mrs. Eva Jones, Omaha

Unique quilts

Mrs. Albert Cloud, Omaha
Mrs. W. R. Stewart, Alliance
Mrs. James Ralmondo, Omaha
Honorable Mention
Mrs. I. L. Stever, Nebraska City
Mrs. A. M. Wilkerson, Lincoln

People drove from miles around
to view the quilt exhibit.

— The Quilts —

—1931—

From mid October 1930 through mid April 1931, the World-Herald printed patterns from the quilt series called Farm Life, designed by Ruby Short McKim. When the last block was printed, an announcement was made that the World-Herald would hold a "quilt making contest" arranged "particularly for the hundreds of women who have been copying the block designs from The Sunday World-Herald each week." There would be prizes awarded for quilts made by older women, by children, by single women and by married women. There would also be a prize for quilts made from block patterns printed in the World-Herald during previous years, and for Antique and Unique quilts.

The quilt show was held June 1 through June 6 on the 10th floor of the Brandeis building. On opening day, 2,000 people came within the first 4 ½ hours to view the 525 quilts entered. "Beauty, Originality Bring High Praise at Exhibit" read the headline. The show proved so popular that it was held over two extra days.

On Memorial Day, May 30, 1931, the Omaha World-Herald ran a photograph and story about a quilt entered in the contest by 71-year-old Mrs. Mary Peck. Mrs. Peck, a resident of Omaha, had traveled to France with other Gold Star Mothers in 1930 to visit the grave of her son, Fred L. Peck, who was killed eight days before the signing of the Armistice. The story of the Gold Star Mothers trip was told in the Omaha World-Herald accompanied by letters sent by Mrs. Peck while onboard the ship *America* on her way to Europe, while she was in France and upon her return to Omaha.

Mrs. Peck made the quilt in honor of her son, calling it "When the Blue Star Turned to Gold." Judging from the photograph, Mrs. Peck's quilt appears to have been bed size. The quilt I have designed is much smaller, and is intended to be hung on a wall or placed on a table. Perhaps you will make this quilt in memory of a family member who made the extreme sacrifice of his or her life for our country. Or, make it to honor all the men and women who have served in the past, or are currently serving their country, so we all may enjoy freedom.

21

When the Blue Star
—Turned to Gold—

FINISHED SIZE: 26" X 26" SQUARE
DESIGNED BY DONNA DI NATALE
PIECED BY MARILYN CARR
QUILTED BY FREDA SMITH

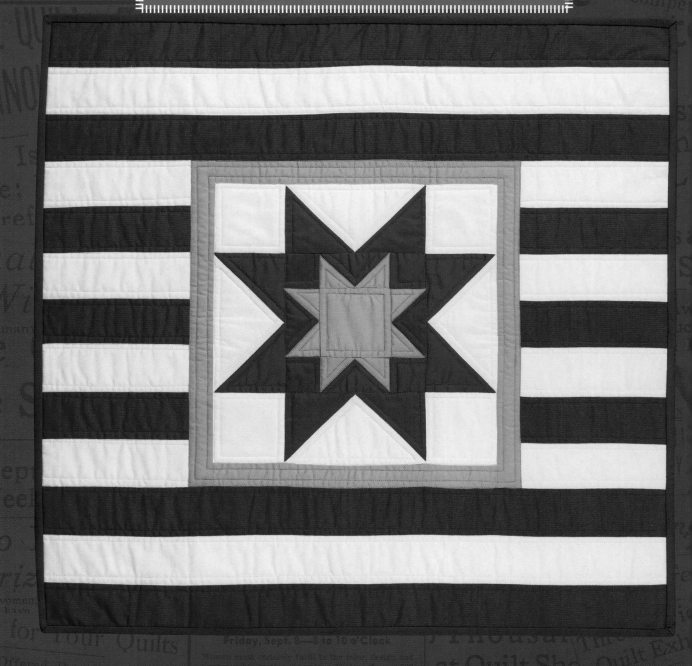

This double 8-point star quilt is based on the quilt made by Mrs. Mary Peck. Mary's quilt bore a gold star for her son. In this quilt, the blue star is in honor of all military personnel, past and present; the gold star is in honor of those who have died while serving in the military. It is square to resemble Mary's quilt, however, you can make it more "flag shaped" by making the stripes longer. Be sure to purchase additional red and white fabric if you decide to do this.

This quilt is dedicated to my uncle, Ralph Simpson (1924-2013), who served aboard the U.S.S. Bunker Hill in WWII.

Fabric and Supplies

- Fat quarter gold for star and frame (minimum 9" x 18")
- ½ yard blue for star and binding
- ½ yard white for star background and stripes
- ⅓ yard red for stripes
- ⅞ yard for backing

Cutting

From the gold, cut:
- 1 – 3 ½" square
- 8 – 2" squares
- 2 – 1 ½" x 12 ½" strips
- 2 – 1 ½" x 14 ½" strips

From the blue, cut:
- 1 – 2" x WOF strip; subcut into 4 – 2" x 3 ½" rectangles and 4 – 2" squares
- 8 – 3 ½" squares
- 3 – 2 ¼" x WOF strips for binding

From the white*, cut:
- 1 – 3 ½" x WOF strip; subcut into 4 – 3 ½" x 6 ½" rectangles and 4 – 3 ½" squares
- 3 – 2 ½" x 13" strips
- 4 – 2 ½" x 26 ½" strips

From the red*, cut:
- 4 – 2 ½" x 13" strips
- 3 – 2 ½" x 26 ½" strips

Tip: From both the red and the white, cut 4 – 2 ½" x width of fabric strips; subcut 3 strips into 1 – 2 ½" x 13" strip and 1 – 2 ½" x 26 ½" strip. Cut the third strip into 1 – 2 ½" x 26 ½" strip.

Gold Star Assembly

Place 1 gold 2" square on 1 blue rectangle and sew diagonally across the square as shown.

Tip: Begin sewing in the center and sew toward the corner. You will have neater and more accurate seams.

Trim the seam to ¼". Open and press the seam toward the blue. Sew a 2" gold square to the other side of the rectangle in the same manner. Make 4 of these units.

Align Sew Trim Press & repeat Trim & press

Sew a Flying Geese unit to each side of the 3 ½" gold square. Press the seams toward the gold square.

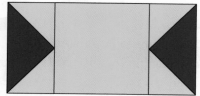

Sew a 2" blue square to each end of the remaining two Flying Geese units. Press the seams toward the blue square.

Sew one of these units to the top and bottom to complete the 6 ½" star. Press the seams away from the center unit.

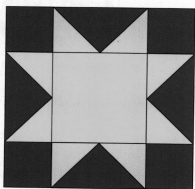

Blue Star Assembly

Make 4 Flying Geese units following the directions for the gold star. Use 1 – 3 ½" x 6 ½" white rectangle and 2 blue 3 ½" squares for each unit.

Sew a unit to each side of the small star block. Press seams toward the small star.

Sew a white 3 ½" square to each end of the remaining Flying Geese units. Press the seams open. Sew one of these units to the top and bottom to complete the 12 ½" star block. Press the seams open.

Gold Frame Assembly

Measure across the center of your block. It should measure 12 ½". Sew a 1 ½" x 12 ½" strip to the top and bottom of the center block. Press the seams toward the gold. Now sew the remaining 2 strips to the sides of the block and press the seams toward the gold. Your center block is now finished.

Stripes Assembly

Sew the 13" red and 13" white strips together alternating colors. Press seams open.

Cut in half to make 2 – 6 ½" x 14 ½" striped rectangles.

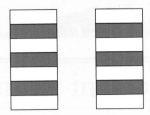

Sew a striped section to each side of the star block.

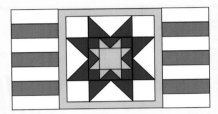

Sew 2 red 2 ½" x 26 ½" strips to 1 white 2 ½" x 26 ½" strip, alternating the colors. Press the seams open. Repeat with the remaining 2 red strips and 1 white strips.

Sew one long striped unit to the top of the star/stripe unit and the other long striped unit to the bottom. Press the seams open.

Check to make sure that your quilt is square. Trim if necessary. The top should measure about 26 ½" square.

Stay-stitch a scant ¼" from the edge along the two sides to keep the seams from opening during quilting.

Quilt and bind.

Optional Star Baby

Using 30s reproduction fabrics changes this quilt into a lovely baby quilt. Marilyn chose to make Star Baby the same size at the Blue Star Turned to Gold quilt, but it can also be made larger by increasing the width of the stripes or adding more stripes.

—1932—

Beginning on September 27, 1931, the World-Herald printed the State Flower quilt block series designed by McKim Studios. One block was printed each week with the final block in the series printed on August 28, 1932. On September 11, the paper announced that readers should get ready for a second big quilt contest to be held October 17-22, with quilts exhibited throughout the entire Thomas Kilpatrick & Company store.

Quilts started pouring in, and within ten days, more than 150 quilts were received. In all, more than 730 quilts were entered. An article dated October 19 estimated the value of the combined quilts at $75,000, a great amount in 1932 dollars. Crowds exceeded all predictions, with an estimated 7,500 people viewing the exhibit on just the first day.

One quilt design mentioned frequently in 1932, and other years, was Sunbonnet Sue. Sue was based on the characters Molly and Mae from *The Sunbonnet Babies' Primer*, by Eulalie Osgood Grover, first published in 1900. There are so many variations on the pattern that it is difficult to determine just which design or designs may have been entered in quilt contests during the 30s.

Sunbonnet Sue's male counterpart is best known as Overall Bill, but was also called Sunbonnet Sam. Sue and Sam can be found participating in activities, alone or together, such as: gardening, fishing and sports; celebrating holidays; and traveling the world. They may be wearing all sorts of clothing from different eras and different countries, but they always sport those big sunbonnets.

—The Sunbonnet Kids—

DESIGNED AND MADE BY DONNA DI NATALE
HAND QUILTED BY DONNA DI NATALE
FINISHED SIZE: 16" X 17 ½"

A majority of the Sunbonnet Sue patterns designed over the decades have been appliqué or appliqué with embroidery. Simple one-color embroidery, such as red work, was also a popular technique for including Sunbonnet kids in quilts, on pillows, curtains, clothing and other textiles. Sue can be found celebrating the holidays, participating in sports, working in the garden, or playing with her cat or dog. She can even be found being very naughty and dead as a doornail on humorous contemporary quilts.

Sue tried to grow up and be a lady. She took many walks on breezy days, taught school, wore fashionable clothing, and in at least one book appeared with a man and young boy presumed to be her husband and son. Sue also comes in all sizes — from 6" to 16".

The Sunbonnet Sue and Overall Sam designs here were created from a combination of patterns from the late 20s and early 30s. They may be used in a small quilt, but would also look nice framed to decorate a child's room. Clothe them in your favorite prints and embellish them with embroidery and buttons. My friend Alex made the tatted flowers that adorn the quilts, but feel free to substitute embroidery, buttons or tiny yo-yos.

Fabric and Supplies

- ▷ 2 Fat quarters for background (1 for Sue and 1 for Sam)
- ▷ Fat quarter or scraps of 3 different fabrics for each block for dress, overalls, shirt and hat
- ▷ Black or brown scrap for shoes
- ▷ Scrap for cat
- ▷ Scrap for dog
- ▷ Fat quarter for borders
- ▷ 2 Fat quarters for backing (1 for Sue and 1 for Sam)
- ▷ Black embroidery floss
- ▷ Ruffled eyelet or lace, buttons and other embellishments of your choice
- ▷ ¼ yard for binding

Cutting and Sewing Instructions

I used the freezer paper method of appliqué. Use the method of your choice. Patterns do not include seam allowance.

Trace, cut and appliqué the pieces onto your background fabric. If using embellishments such as lace or eyelet, place these under the bottom edge of the appliquéd dress. The ribbon on Sue's bonnet was stitched in place after the hat was appliquéd. Turn the ends of the ribbon under and stitch in place. The braid on Sam's bonnet was made by braiding three pieces of 6-ply embroidery floss. Tie a knot at both ends of the braid. Leave ½" to ¾" of loose thread at the end and tuck the beginning knot under the hat. Stitch in place with straight stitches or zigzag stitch over the braid.

Referring to the photograph, embroider the edges and details using 2 strands of black embroidery floss.

Lay the appliquéd block upside down on a terry towel and press. I like to spray it with Best Press to make sure all the wrinkles are gone from the muslin.

*Trim the fabric to 13" x 14 ½". Be sure the appliqué is centered when you trim.

Cut your borders 2 ¼" wide. I mitered my corners so I cut them all 2 ¼" x 18". If you do not want to miter your corners, cut 2 borders 2 ¼" x 14 ½" and the other 2 borders 2 ¼" x 16 ½" (or the height and width of your appliquéd piece).

If you wish to quilt your block, do so at this time. I hand quilted around Sue and Sam and then quilted a ½" diagonal grid.

Cut 3 - 2 ¼" WOF strips of binding fabric. Sew the strips together.

Bind and enjoy.

Add buttons if desired.

*These would also be cute framed. If you want to frame them, do not trim the fabric. I recommend wrapping plain white or cream fabric around matt board or a piece of foam core (both available at art or craft stores) that is slightly smaller than the size of your frame. Glue the fabric to the board, smoothing the corners as much as possible. Center your appliqué on the board and wrap the extra fabric around to the back. Glue the fabric to the back, trimming first if you wish. Spray the framed block with Scotch Guard and do not cover it with glass.

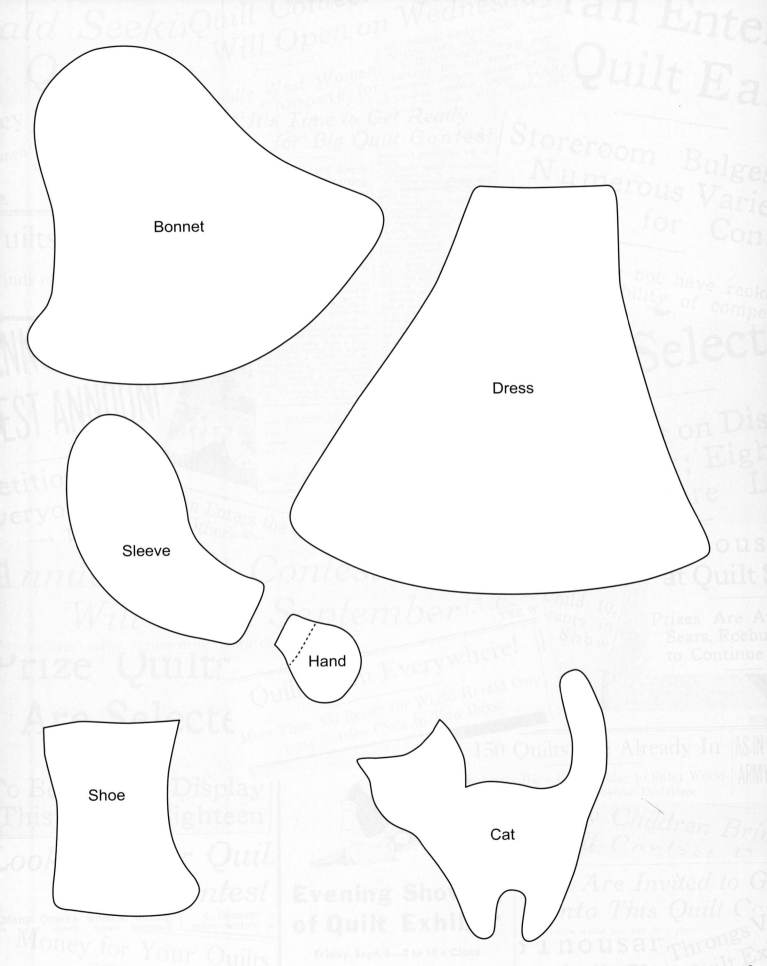

Bonnet

Dress

Sleeve

Hand

Shoe

Cat

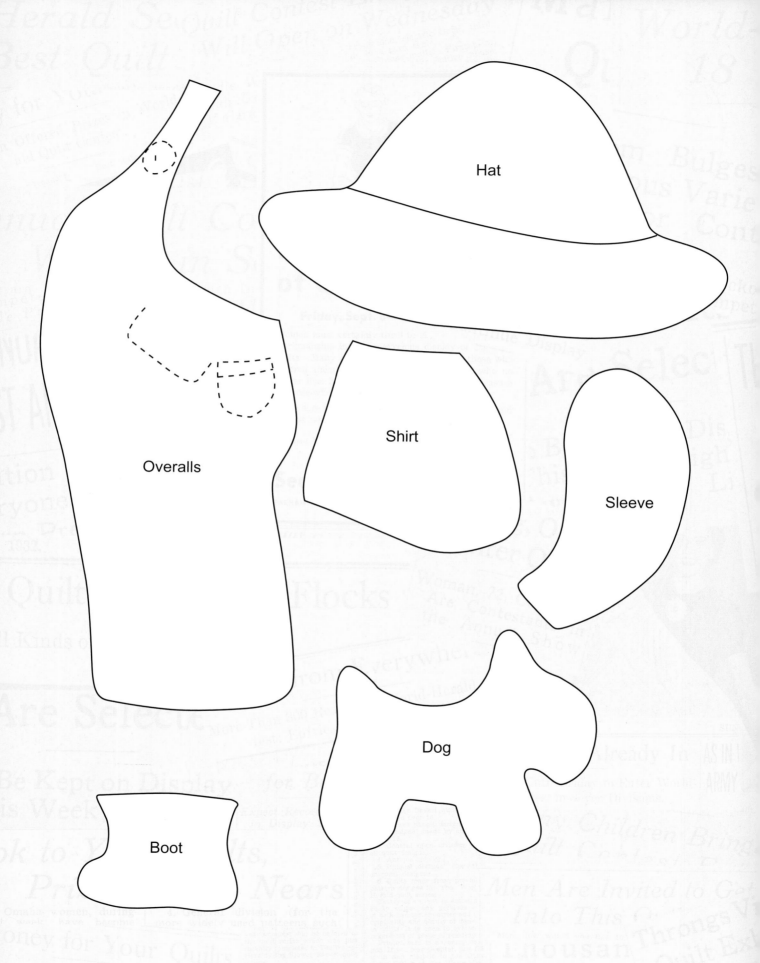

Hat

Overalls

Shirt

Sleeve

Dog

Boot

—1933—

When one thinks of the depression and the dust bowl, 1933 is the defining year. One of every three people was out of work. Due to soil erosion, 2.5 million people were no longer able to earn a living from the land and hundreds of thousands lost their farms and homes. Many loaded up what possessions would fit in and on their vehicle and traveled the country looking for work.

Among the possessions most felt essential were a sewing machine and quilts. Quilts were used as bedding, of course, but also as walls for privacy and packing for fragile items. As these quilts wore out, new quilts were sewn from worn clothing and feed sacks. Yes, this was the era when sugar, flour, salt, animal feed and other commodities came packed in cotton sacks.

Initially, cotton bags were made of plain, unbleached cotton. Women saved these bags and used them for diapers and undergarments, or dyed them for other uses. Some even saved the thread that the bags were sewn with as it was good cotton thread and could be used for crocheted or knit doilies or trims. Soon bag manufacturers realized that women were using these sacks for clothing and household furnishings, and saw an opportunity to increase sales by marketing their cotton bags in colorful prints and solids to match fashion trends.

As more and more manufacturers caught on to this trend, other commodities were packaged in cotton sacks. Books and patterns for making garments from feed sacks were published and women became a driving force when it came to purchasing feed and flour for the family. The kind and size of produce on the shopping list often depended on the item she wanted to sew.

A 5-lb. bag measured 13-15" x 14-19" — a bit smaller than today's fat quarter. A 100-lb. bag measured 36-39" x 42-44", or about 1 1/3 yards. Women would often trade sacks in order to have enough fabric for a dress. Two 100-lb. bags were enough to make almost any garment and leftover scraps were made into quilts.

In October 1933, the World-Herald offered this bright pattern that would have made good use of feed sack scraps. Dig into your stash of 30s prints and have fun paper piecing this prized Rose Point quilt.

SEWING WITH *Cotton Bags*

—Paper Pieced Rose Point—

PIECED BY DONNA DI NATALE
QUILTED BY JANIECE CLINE
FINISHED SIZE: 50" X 50"
FINISHED BLOCK SIZE: 12" (4 – 6" BLOCKS)

The original Rose Point pattern was advertised in the Omaha World-Herald on Oct. 3, 1933. The block pattern was available for 10 cents, or for 40 cents you could order the block pattern, quilting design (No. 542) and the patchwork border pattern (No. 805). Rose Point was one of "over 200" of the most popular designs in the 32-page *Colonial Quilt Book*. The book (or catalog) could be ordered from the Needle Art Department for 25 cents and you would receive one free quilt pattern with each order.

This pattern was also published in the book *Quilt Lover's Delight* by Aunt Martha's Studios, and is still available from Colonial Patterns (colonialpatterns.com).

The original Rose Point pattern came with templates for the diamonds and odd shaped background. I don't really care for set-in seams, so I changed the pattern to a paper-pieced block. If you've never made a paper-pieced quilt, this is a good pattern to start. You will also notice that the pieced circle in the center is now a solid circle that is appliquéd after the block is finished. You could also use a yo-yo in the center.

This was a very fun quilt to make and it was hard to stop at just 9 blocks. For a larger size quilt, simply add more blocks or an extra border or two.

Fabric and Supplies

▷ 3 ¼ yards white or light small print for background and outer border
▷ 1 ¾ yards green print for roses, ruched border and binding
▷ Scraps (minimum 2 ½" x 5" each) colorful prints for rose buds
▷ Fat quarter or 3" square scraps yellow print for circles
▷ 3 ¼ yards for backing
▷ Cotton crochet thread (such as J. P. Coats Knit-Cro Sheen)

Cutting

Pre-cutting pieces for paper piecing is up to the piecer. Some like to cut and work with squares or rectangles; some like to cut pieces close to the actual size and shape of the pattern piece. And then others like to work with strips and scraps of fabric. Cutting instructions given here are for squares or rectangles that will fit in the required space with plenty of room for seam allowances.

From the white small print, cut:

▷ 12 – 6 ½" x WOF strips; subcut into 144 - 6 ½" x 3 ¼" rectangles. (A2, A3, B4 and B5)
▷ 5 – 7" x WOF strips* for outer border

From the green print, cut:

▷ 4 – 5 ½" x WOF strips; subcut into 36 – 5 ½" x 4 ½" rectangles. (A1)
▷ 5 – 3" x WOF strips; subcut into 72 – 3" x 2 ¼" rectangles. (B2 and B3)
▷ 4 – 1 ½" x WOF strips for ruched inner border
▷ 6 – 2 ¼" x WOF strips for binding

From the colorful prints, cut:

▷ 36 – 2 ½" x 4 ¾" rectangles (B1)

From the yellow print, cut:

▷ 9 circles (C)

*This border actually finishes at 6" but I like to cut my borders 1" wider than the finished width. This allows just a tad extra for the machine quilter to grab onto. When I squared up my quilt after it was quilted, I used the border seams as a guide, and cut the width to 6 ¼".

Assembly

Photocopy or trace the patterns on page 40 onto your favorite foundation paper. You will need 36 copies of each pattern for the entire quilt (4 of each per block).

Using your preferred method for paper piecing, make 36 of pieced triangle A and 36 of pieced triangle B. Stitch A and B together on marked line to make 1 block. Referring to the quilt photograph, stitch 4 blocks together to create the 12" finished Rose Point block. Appliqué the yellow circle or yo-yo to the center of the block. Make 9 Rose Point blocks.

Sew the Rose Point blocks together into three rows of three blocks each. The quilt top center should measure 36 ½" square.

Inner Border

The inner border is gathered into what is termed a ruched border. This adds a nice texture to the quilt and really frames the Rose Point blocks.

Cut 8 pieces of crochet thread approximately 55" long. The exact length isn't crucial, but you must have sufficient thread at each end of the border strip to pull on in order to create the gathers.

Set your sewing machine to a long and wide zigzag stitch that will stitch over the crochet thread and not through it.

Place one of the 1 ½" x WOF inner border strips

in your machine with the pressure foot on the very edge of the wrong side of the fabric. You want your zigzag stitches to be at the edge of the fabric but not overlap the edge.

Holding the crochet thread in your left hand behind the pressure foot, place the crochet thread between the toes of the pressure foot. Drop your pressure foot. Take 1 or 2 stitches by turning the wheel by hand. Is the zigzag stitch wide enough so that the stitches are on either side of the crochet thread? If not, adjust the width of the stitch.

Slowly zigzag over the crochet thread all the way to the end of the strip. Go slowly and make sure you do not stitch through the crochet thread. Leave 4"–6" of thread on each end.

Do this on both sides of all 4 inner border strips.

Find the center of the inner border strip and place a pin there. Find the center of one side of the quilt top and place a pin there. Pin the border strip to the quilt top matching centers and each end.

To gather the border strip, start at one end and pull on the crochet thread that is nearest the pinned edge. While doing this, move the gathers toward the center of the strip. When the gathers have reached the center of the strip, move to the opposite end and pull the crochet thread on that end. Again, smooth the gathers toward the center. The gathers will not be very full so don't over-gather the strips. Do this until the gathered strip measures the same as your quilt top (roughly 36 ½"). Pin the rest of the border to the top, spreading the gathers out evenly along the length and making sure the top is smooth with no gaps or puckers.

Tip: Place a pin through the thread at each end to keep the gathers from slipping.

Sew the inner border to the quilt top using a ¼" seam. (Be sure to change back to a regular straight stitch.) The gathering stitches and crochet thread should both be within the seam allowance. I found it easier to do this with the gathered border down, against the machine, and the quilt top up. The border strip will want to wander a bit, so pin liberally and go slowly when you stitch to keep your seam even. Remember to take the pins out as you reach them.

Repeat on the other side and then on the top and bottom. Start and stop the top and bottom borders at the end of the gathered side borders, just as you would for a non-gathered border.

When all for inner borders are attached, gather the outer edge of each strip by pulling on the other crochet thread and evenly smoothing the gathers. Make sure the outer edge of the border is the same length as the inner edge.

Measure across the width and length at the center. Your top should now measure about 38 ½" square.

Outer Border

Cut 2 – 7" x 38 ½" strips and 2 – 7" x 51 ½" strips.

Take one of the 38 ½" border strips and fold it in half. Finger press or pin to mark the center. Measure to find the center of one side and mark with a pin.

Pin the outer border to the inner border, matching centers and ends. Adjust the gathers so that there are no gaps or puckers in the outer border. Sew a ¼"

seam, being careful to keep the gathers smooth and even and the zigzag stitches inside the seam allowance.

Repeat on the opposite side of your quilt top with the other short outer border.

Attach the remaining two outer border pieces to the top and bottom of your quilt. After the outer borders are securely sewn, you can go back and trim the ends of the crochet threads or remove the threads if you can. If any of the zigzag stitching shows in the inner border, remove those stitches by carefully clipping them.

Finishing

Ruched sashing or borders are a bit of a challenge to some machine quilters. The best way to treat them is by stitching in the ditch.

Quilt, bind and enjoy.

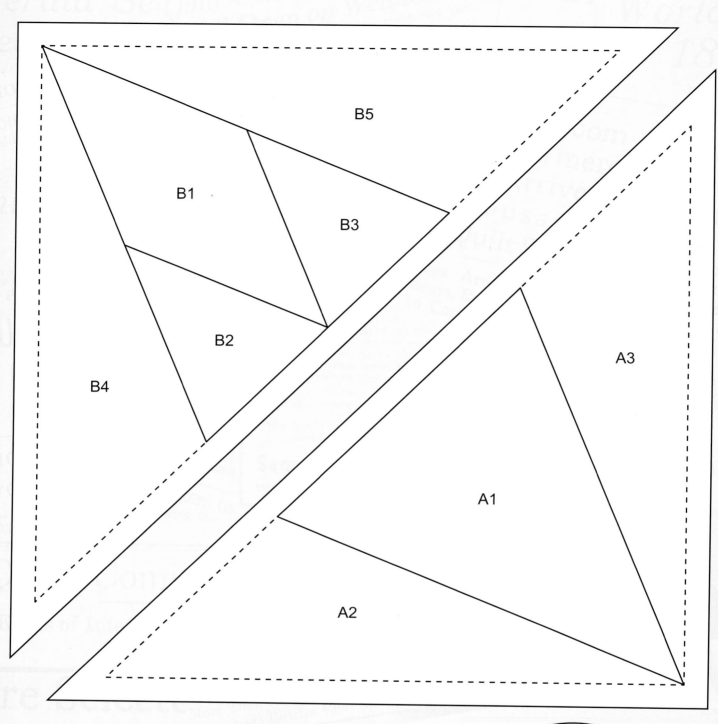

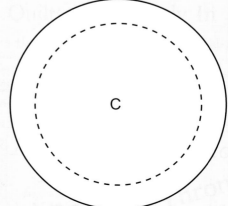

—1934—

*T*he drought that ravaged the plains states continued into 1934 with record-setting temperatures well into the 100s. People sought relief from the heat under shade trees, on their front porch and in cool basement rooms, where one could stitch a quilt for the contest that was to be held come September. When the show opened, Union Outfitting, the host store and co-sponsor of the contest, opened their doors for an evening viewing. More than 1,200 people crowded the store that first evening to see the many quilts displayed on the store's five floors, in air-conditioned comfort.

For the Omaha World-Herald quilt contest, 1934 turned out to be a year of many numbers, especially the number of pieces in a single quilt. One woman submitted a quilt made of more than 8,000 pieces. Mrs. L. F. Wollen of Wilsonville, Nebraska, entered a quilt that had 175 blocks, all of them different, made of 8,405 pieces. A quilt sent in by L. A. Coleman, of Superior, Nebraska, contained 9,999 pieces, and the editor challenged readers to surpass the 10,000 piece mark.

Mrs. C. M. Wilson, Omaha, entered a quilt containing 11,700 pieces that had been made more than 100 years before. The quilt was described as, "Tiny strips of varied-colored material pieced together in an almost triangle form." A few days later a "house quilt" was submitted that contained 13,500 pieces. I wonder who counted all of those pieces! I think we can assume that the editor and judges trusted the owner and did not bother with a recount.

One unique quilt from this year was made of 620 tobacco sacks, entered by Mrs. August Blaszak of Omaha. Mrs. Blaszak stated that she had "ripped, washed and ironed" every one of those sacks before sewing them into a quilt.

Of all the numbers published, the total number of quilts entered in 1934 was never mentioned, but from these articles one can imagine the amazing display of colorful prized quilts.

In keeping with the numbers theme, I chose to use the Tumbler block, sometimes called the Thimble block, for this quilt of many pieces. This is one of those patterns that can be made as small or as large as you wish. It all depends on the size of the pieces and the number of pieces.

—A Quilt of Many Pieces—

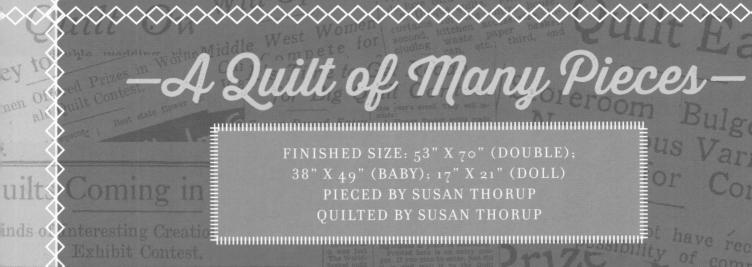

FINISHED SIZE: 53" X 70" (DOUBLE);
38" X 49" (BABY); 17" X 21" (DOLL)
PIECED BY SUSAN THORUP
QUILTED BY SUSAN THORUP

$\mathcal{T}$he Tumbler block, while old, is also seen in modern quilts. The larger sizes can be used to show off big, bold prints or can be worked into soft flannel "rag" quilts. Several rulers and templates for cutting this shape are available. This pattern uses the EZ Fat Cats ruler by Darlene Zimmerman, or you may use the templates provided. The EZ Fat Cats ruler is nice because it can be used to make blocks from 1" to 11 ½" tall.

The baby quilt and larger quilt both use 4" tumblers while the doll quilt uses 2" tumblers. Of course, you may use the 2" tumblers to make larger quilts if you want. The size is determined by the number of blocks. How many pieces can you sew into your Quilt of Many Pieces?

Fabric and Supplies

Double

- 18 – ¼ yard cuts or fat quarters (or 430 – 4" squares) of various fabric for Tumblers
- ⅝ yard for binding
- 3 ½ yards for backing

Baby

- 12 – ¼ yard cuts or 12 fat quarters (or 210 – 4" squares) of various fabric for Tumblers
- ½ yard for binding
- 1 ½ yard for backing

Doll

- 11 Fat Eighths (or 182 – 2" squares) of various fabric for Tumblers
- ¼ yard for binding
- ⅞ yard for backing

All

- EZ Fat Cats ruler from EZ Quilting or template plastic

Cutting

Double and Baby Quilts

Instructions are given for the double size quilt with instructions for the baby quilt in parenthesis.

Cut 2 – 4" x width of fabric strips from each fabric for a total of at least 36 (20) strips. If using fat quarters, cut 4 (3) – 4" x 22" from each fat quarter for a total of 72 (36) strips.

Using the Fat Cat ruler, place the ruler at the 1 ½" and 5 ½" markings as shown, to make the 4" tumblers. – OR – Use the large template on page 47. Make six cuts, alternating the position of the ruler/template as you move across the fabric. Repeat this step for each fabric. You will need a total of 420 (210) tumblers.

Doll Quilt

Cut 2 – 2" x width of fabric strips from each piece of fabric. If using fat eighths, cut 11 – 2" strips. Using the Fat Cat ruler, place the narrow end of the ruler on one edge of the 2" strip. The upper edge of the fabric should line up with the 2" mark on the ruler. – OR – Use the small template on page 47. Cut out the tumblers, alternating the position of the ruler as you move across the fabric. You will need a total of 182 tumblers.

Sewing

All sizes

Lay out as many tumblers as you can fit on your design wall or a large flat surface, alternating the direction of the tumblers. Arrange the tumblers to achieve a pleasing mix of colors and prints. Stack the pieces in order and pin and number each row to keep them in order. You can also take a picture of the layout to guide you in putting the tumblers and rows together.

Sew the tumblers together as shown. Place the wide edge of one tumbler face down on the narrow edge of the next tumbler. The top and bottom of the tumblers will not match, but should cross ¼" from the outer edge.

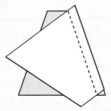

Sew 21 (15) tumbler blocks together, alternating edges as shown. This makes one row.

Repeat to make a total of 20 (14) rows.

Press all the seams in the same direction. Every other row will be turned upside down for the sewing the rows together. By pressing all the seams in the same direction, the seams will nest when turned.

Sew the rows together as shown. The side edges of the rows will zigzag back and forth and will be trimmed after all the rows are sewn together.

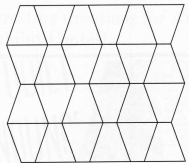

Finishing

Using the longest and widest ruler you have, lay your ruler on one zigzag side, aligning the bottom of your ruler with the bottom of the quilt and the side edge of the ruler with the narrowest point of the rows. You now have a nice rectangular top.

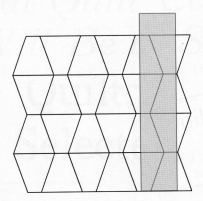

Quilt, bind and enjoy.

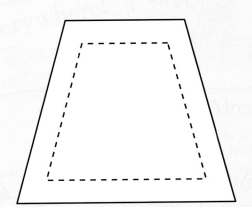

—1935—

This was a big year for the World-Herald quilt contest; more than 700 quilts were entered. It took more than two full floors of the Sears building to display quilts in the General Open category alone!

The Flower Basket pattern series, designed by Ruby Short McKim, was the focus of the 1935 contest. Beautiful flowers of many hues appliquéd onto pieced blocks, sewn together and set on point, would have made a very colorful display, but there may not have been a lot of quilts from this series entered into the contest. The flowers in the blocks are very detailed, using small, irregularly shaped pieces, and embellished with embroidery. The ability to finish one of these quilts in time for the contest would have presented a challenge. Thus, the Flower Basket quilts were displayed on one floor along with quilts made by children, antique quilts and unique quilts.

Other floral patterns were also popular during this time, including several tulip patterns. The Royal Dutch Tulip, Dutch Tulip No. 131 and The Dutch Tulip were all offered for sale by sending 10 to 40 cents to the Needle Art Editor at the World-Herald. The Dutch Tulip, given here, was evidently quite popular as it was advertised in three different years between 1930 and 1940.

The Dutch Tulip pattern could be ordered for 10 cents from the Omaha World-Herald Needle Art Department, 243 West 17th Street, in New York City. True to its creative history, as of July 2013, the building at this address is listed as a Creative Loft space that can be rented for $2,814 per month. That is about two-and-a-half times what the average worker earned all year in 1935.

ARY 11, 1941.

Dutch Tulip

Dutch tulip quilt has only two patches to applique and it's your chance to use up those print scraps to good advantage. Finish with a bit of outline stitch. Pattern 6678 contains the block chart; carefully drawn pattern pieces; color schemes; directions for quilt; yardage chart; illustration of quilt.

Write plainly name, address and pattern number and send with 10 cents in coin to The World-Herald Needle Art Department, 243 West Seventeenth street, New York City. Allow eight days for delivery. When

COPR. 1940, HOUSEHOLD ARTS, INC.

PATTERN 6678 ordering be sure to give correct number, as patterns cannot be exchanged when order is filled according to instructions.

—Scrappy Dutch Tulip—

DESIGNED AND MADE BY DONNA DI NATALE
QUILTED BY DAVID HURD
FINISHED QUILT SIZE: 60" SQUARE
FINISHED BLOCK SIZE: 8" SQUARE

Of the various tulip patterns printed in the paper, this one is my favorite. It is whimsical and perfect for using lots of 30s reproduction fabrics. I wanted to include both solids and prints, so I changed the flowers from one piece to two pieces. I used Moda Bella Solids for the plain fabrics. This fabric comes in so many colors that I had no problem coming up with 25 different colors to match my 25 prints. I even used different colors of greens for the leaves. The sashing on this quilt is narrow to give it the look of flowers blooming through a trellis or an old-fashioned multi-paned window.

Fabric and Supplies

- ▷ 1 $^{7}/_{8}$ yards white or off-white solid for background
- ▷ Scraps of 25 assorted prints* for tulips
- ▷ Scraps of 25 assorted solids to coordinate with prints*
- ▷ 7 fat quarters of assorted green solids to coordinate with the flower fabrics**
- ▷ 1 yard gold print for sashing and inner border
- ▷ 1 $^{1}/_{4}$ yards green for outer border
- ▷ 3 yards for backing
- ▷ 2 yards light-weight fusible webbing

*each flower (2 pieces) can be cut from a 3 $^{1}/_{2}$" x 4 $^{1}/_{2}$" scrap

**a piece of fabric 7" x 15" is enough for 6 leaves

Cutting

From the white, cut:

- ▷ 25 – 8 $^{1}/_{2}$" squares
- ▷ 2 – 6 $^{5}/_{8}$" squares; cut once diagonally for corner triangles
- ▷ 3 – 12 $^{5}/_{8}$" squares; cut twice diagonally for side setting triangles

From the gold print, cut:

- ▷ 8 – 1" x WOF strips; subcut into 32 – 8 $^{1}/_{2}$" strips for block sashing
- ▷ 8 – 1" x WOF strips for row sashing
- ▷ 5 – 1" x WOF strips for inner border
- ▷ 6 – 2 $^{1}/_{4}$" x WOF strips for binding

From the green, cut:

- ▷ 6 – 6" x WOF strips for outer border

Note: The templates and instructions for this quilt are for fused raw edge machine appliqué. If you wish to use another method of appliqué, you may need to add a seam allowance to each piece.

Before You Sew

Trace the templates on page 54 onto the paper side of the fusible webbing. Leave at least $^{1}/_{4}$" between pieces.

You will need 50 tulips, 50 petals and 25 leaves but make a few extra for a practice block or in case one of them decides to go walk about. Trace up to half the pieces in reverse to add variety to the blocks.

Cut fusible pieces about 1/8" outside the drawn line. Cut out the center of each piece, leaving 1/8" to $^{1}/_{4}$" of fusible inside the drawn line.

Fuse the pieces to the reverse of your selected fabrics. To replicate the quilt shown here, cut out a back and center flower piece from each print and coordinating solid. You will need a total of 25 print flowers and 25 solid flowers. I also used a variety of greens for the leaves.

Cut out each fused piece on the drawn line. Now you are ready to assemble your blocks.

Assemble The Blocks

Fuse the leaf to the 8 ½" background squares, placing the bottom point of the leaf in the lower corner of the square, matching raw edges.

Fuse the flowers to either the right or the left of the leaf, depending on which way the leaf is turned. (See placement guide.) The flowers do not need to be placed exactly according to the guide, and in fact, they do not have to be placed exactly alike in each block. You may want to lay out several blocks before fusing to see what looks best.

Fuse the background flower first and then fuse the petal on top. I alternated the print and solid centers, so that the print flowers had a solid petal and vice versa. This is a scrappy quilt, so mix things up as much as you want.

I used a straight stitch and sewed just inside the outer edge of each appliqué piece. You may use any stitch you like. Using a blanket or buttonhole stitch and black thread makes a more authentic looking 30s quilt, but I like to match my thread to the appliqué pieces.

Tip: if using matching thread, sew all of one color before moving on to the next color. This saves time switching out the top thread. Use bobbin thread to match your background fabric.

When you have all 25 blocks fused and pressed, place them on a design wall or lay them out on a table. Arrange the blocks in a pleasing color

pattern. If you have a design wall, you can leave them on the wall and take them down a row at a time. If you don't have a design wall, or even if you do, take a photograph of your layout to use as a reference when assembling the quilt.

This quilt is set on point, so the first row has only 1 appliqué block and 2 setting triangles. The next row has 3 appliqué blocks, the next 5, the next 7 and then back to 5, 3, 1.

Sashing

Now it's time to attach the sashing and assemble the quilt. Following the assembly guide, sew the 8 ½" sashing strips between the blocks first. Add another 8 ½" sashing strip to each end then attach the setting triangles to the ends of each row. Stitch together the 7 – 1" row sashing strips into one long strip. Subcut the long strip into 2 – 12" strips, 2 – 30" strips, 2 – 45" strips and 2 – 63" strips. (The sashing strips between the rows are cut longer than needed.) Stitch the rows and row sashing strips together. Leave extra sashing on each end to be trimmed. Stitch the oversized 12" sashing strips to the two remaining corners. Attach the corner triangles. Trim to square up the quilt.

Tip: This quilt uses very narrow sashing strips. I think this is more difficult than wider strips, but I wanted the sashing to look like a trellis with the flowers peaking out in between the strips. My best advice is to sew slowly and make sure your seams are straight and even scant ¼" seams.

Inner Border

The first border is simply the same sashing strip sewn on all four sides of the quilt.

Measure across the middle of your top. Mine measured 48 ½". Stitch together and trim 1" inner border strips to make 2 strips this length.

Sew an inner border strip to one side of your top. Sew a second strip to the opposite side of your top.

Measure your top again, from side to side including the side borders. Mine measured 49 ½". Stitch together and trim 1" inner border strips to make 2 strips this length.

Sew one strip to the top and the other to the bottom of your quilt.

Outer Border

Time to measure again. This should be a no-brainer, but measure anyway; it's a good habit to get into. Measure the width across the middle (your top is square so it doesn't matter where you measure as long as it is across the middle). Mine measured 49 ½".

Stitch together and trim 6" border strips to make 2 strips this length. Sew one border to two opposing sides of the quilt top.

Measure your top again, from side to side including the side borders. Mine measured 60 ½". Stitch together and trim 1" inner border strips to make 2 strips this length. Sew one to the top and one to the bottom of your top.

Measure again – JUST KIDDING! You are actually done with your quilt top.

Quilt, bind and enjoy!

53

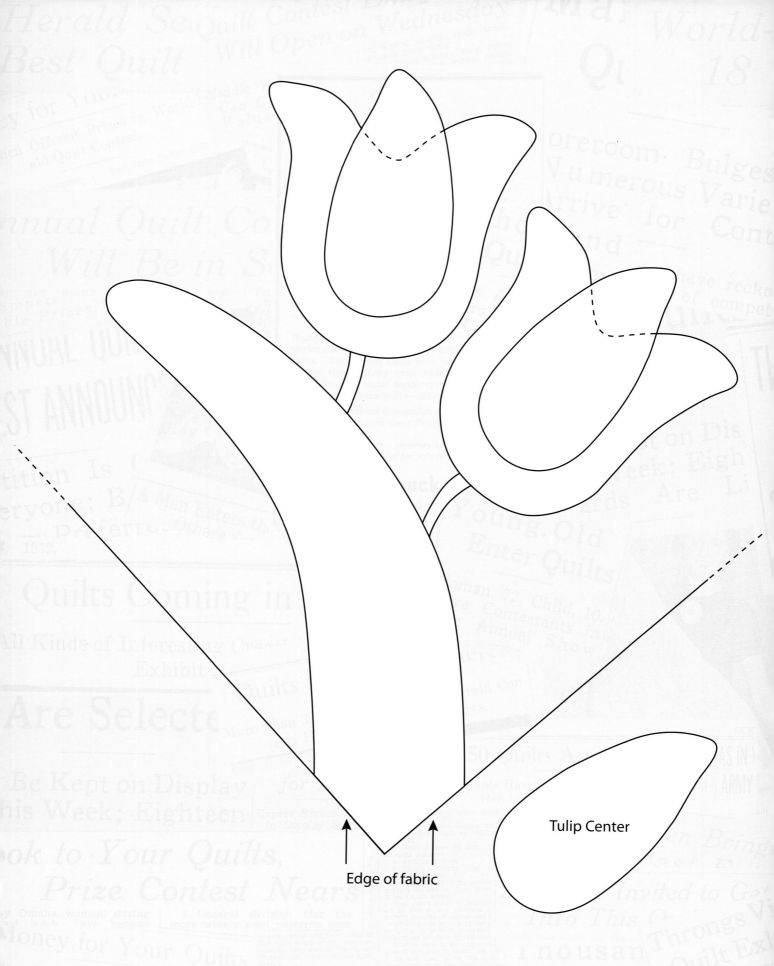

Edge of fabric

Tulip Center

—1936—

Flowers have always been a popular subject for quilts and quilt patterns, but in the 1920s and 3os, the addition of butterflies gave floral patterns a new, more whimsical personality.

The majority of butterfly quilts are appliquéd, although you do find embroidered butterflies and the occasional pieced butterfly. The butterflies could be large, small, viewed from on top or from the side. They could be realistic or very stylized. At times the quilter would try to replicate the actual coloration of the butterfly, but in most cases, any print was fair game.

In 1935, Mrs. Henry Field, of Henry Field's Seed Company in Shenandoah, Iowa, entered a butterfly quilt in the World-Herald contest. Mrs. Field did not win a prize, but I still thought it appropriate to have a butterfly quilt to represent this year.

But which butterfly pattern? So many different ones were available through newspaper and magazine ads. In 2012, I purchased a pink and white version of this quilt at an antique mall in Omaha, Nebraska. So I thought this is the perfect pattern: an Omaha quilt in an "Omaha" book.

As it turned out, Susan Thorup, who works at Prairie Point Quilts and Fabric in Shawnee, Kansas, had also purchased a yellow and white butterfly quilt, made from the same pattern as mine. She liked it so much that she made a pattern to sell in the shop. Susan was more than happy to allow me to include "our" quilt in this book. After all, how many times do you run into someone with a nearly identical vintage quilt? It was meant to be.

Butterflies and flowers not only adorned quilts in the 3os. Many household items such as pillows, rugs, curtains, tablecloths, tea towels, potholders and even clothing, sported the delightful designs. How many ways can you think of to use this butterfly throughout your home?

—Butterflies—

DESIGNED AND MADE BY SUSAN THORUP
FINISHED SIZE: 63 ½" X 76"
FINISHED BLOCK SIZE: 9"

*T*his butterfly pattern is one of the easiest to appliqué and is included here in hopes that anyone who "doesn't appliqué" will give it a try. The butterfly is cut from one piece of fabric — no separate wings or body to sew in place. Details are then embroidered, something that is quite common in butterfly quilts. I don't know of anyone who wants to appliqué 1/16" antennae on their butterflies.

The blocks in this quilt are set on point. I feel this gives the butterflies movement across the quilt. Of course you may certainly use a square setting if you prefer, and adjust the number of blocks accordingly.

The scalloped edge simply adds to the light and airy feeling of this quilt. Using the Easy Scallop tool by Darlene Zimmerman makes the scalloped edge a snap.

These instructions are for fused raw-edge machine appliqué. The templates do not include a seam allowance.

Fabric and Supplies

- ▷ 2 yards white, off white or light color for background
- ▷ 4 yards yellow for alternate squares, setting triangles, outer border and binding
- ▷ 20 fat quarters or 10" squares for butterflies
- ▷ 4 ½ yards for backing
- ▷ Lightweight fusible webbing
- ▷ Embroidery floss in black
- ▷ Template plastic or stiff cardboard
- ▷ Easy Scallop tool from EZ Quilting if making the scalloped edge.
- ▷ Removable or wash-out marking pen or pencil

Cutting

From the white, cut:

- ▷ 20 – 10 ½" squares (these will be trimmed to 9 ½" after being embroidered)
- ▷ 7 – 1 ¾" x WOF strips for inner border

From the yellow, cut:

- ▷ 12 – 9 ½" squares
- ▷ 4 – 14 ½" squares; cut diagonally twice for side triangles
- ▷ 2 – 8 ½" squares; cut diagonally once for corner triangles
- ▷ 8 – 5 ½" x WOF strips for outer border
- ▷ 1 – 24" square; cut into 1 ¼" bias strips for single fold bias binding

Sewing

Trace the butterfly template on page 62 onto template plastic or stiff cardboard — something that won't lose its shape when traced over and over. Cut out on the traced line.

Trace the butterflies onto the paper side of fusible webbing. Trace 20 butterflies.

Roughly cut out each butterfly at least ⅛" outside the drawn line.

Iron the fusible webbing to the wrong side of the print fabrics according to the manufacturer's directions.

Optional: before fusing, cut out the center of the butterfly, leaving ¼" to ½" of webbing around the edge.

Cut out each butterfly on the traced line. Remove the paper backing.

Trace the embroidery lines on the right side of the fabric using a removable pen or pencil.

Position a butterfly on each of the 10 ½" squares. Be sure to leave space at the top for the antennae. Fuse the butterfly to the block according to the manufacturer's instructions.

Draw the antennae on the butterflies.

Optional: machine stitch just inside the edge of the butterflies using a straight stitch. This double secures the butterflies to the background fabric.

Embroider the butterflies using a small running stitch across the butterfly and a stem stitch for the antennae. Use a blanket stitch around the outer edge of the butterfly.

Press the blocks on the reverse side.

Trim each block to 9 ½" keeping the butterfly centered on the block.

Assembling The Blocks

Use your design wall or a flat surface to lay out your butterfly blocks, alternate squares and setting triangles. Refer to the assembly diagram for placement. This quilt does not have sashing, so when you are pleased with your arrangement, it is time to sew.

Sew the triangles and blocks together into diagonal rows. The triangles are oversized to allow for wriggle room.

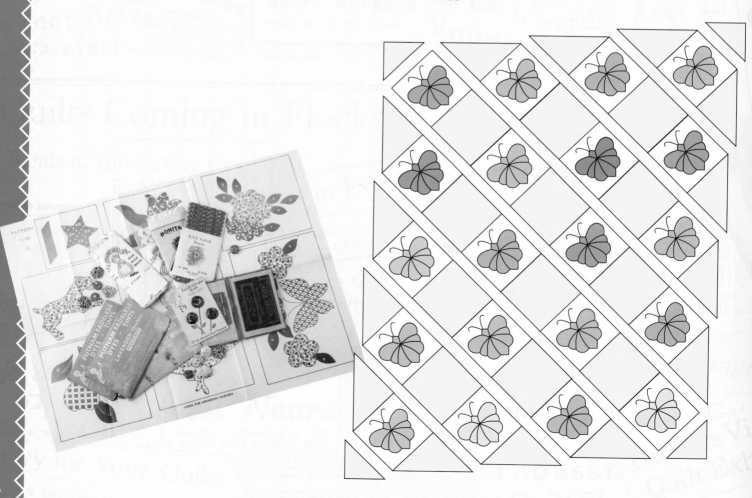

Press all seams toward the alternate blocks.

Sew the rows together.

Add the 4 corner triangles. Square and trim the corners and all four sides.

Measure the width and length of your top through the middle. The top should measure about 51 ½" x 64".

Inner Border

Piece 2 white inner border strips together. Cut 2 strips 64" or the length of your quilt top. Cut the other 2 strips 54" or the width of your top after attaching the side borders.

Your quilt top should measure 54" x 66 ½".

Outer Border

Sew two border strips together to make one long strip. Remember to cut off the selvage edges before piecing the strips together. Repeat. Make 4 border strips.

Cut 2 border strips 66 ½" long, or the length of your quilt top. Sew one outer border strip to each side of your quilt top. Carefully press the seams toward the borders.

Measure the width of the top across the middle, including the outer border strips. It should measure about 64". Trim the 2 remaining outer border strips to this measurement.

Sew an outer border strip to the top and bottom. Carefully press the seams toward the borders.

Scalloped Edge

You can use a dinner plate or other round object to mark your scallops, but Susan used the Easy Scallop tool to mark the edges because it makes it so easy to calculate the width of the scallop.

To duplicate this quilt, mark 6 scallops on the sides and 5 scallops on the top and bottom. Set the larger scallop tool at the 8 ¾" mark. Begin by centering and marking each corner according to the Easy Scallop instructions. Then mark the sides. Use a marking pencil or chalk that does not rub off easily. It will be handled quite a bit before you add the binding, and you want the marks to remain until then.

Note: mark your top before you quilt it. The mark will tell you or your quilter where to stop quilting.

Do not cut the scallops yet.

Quilt or have someone else complete the quilting at this point. Make sure they understand that the edge is to be scalloped. Show them the marks so they can follow the edge or stop the quilting inside the line.

Binding

If you have used the Easy Scallop tool, follow the binding instructions that come with the tool.

Otherwise, carefully trim the quilt on the marked scallop line. Attach the binding, easing over the outer curve and clipping in the V in between the scallops.

Your quilt is finished and ready to enjoy!

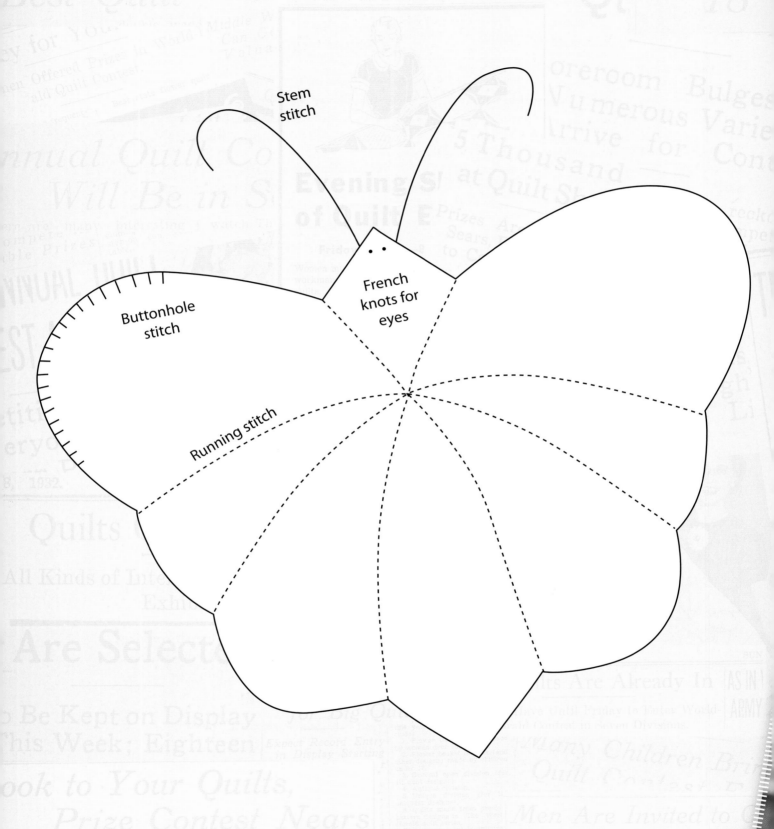

Stem stitch

French knots for eyes

Buttonhole stitch

Running stitch

—1937—

Quilts Woven Into History

Feb. 14, 1937, brought a new series to the Omaha World-Herald. This series, called Quilts Woven into History, was based in the renewed interest in old patchwork quilt designs. The series included 12 pieced blocks:

▷ Railroad Crossing
▷ Charlotte's Crown
▷ Indian Trail
▷ Clay's Choice

▷ Dolly Madison Star
▷ 54-40 Fight
▷ Crossroads
▷ Free Trade

▷ Prairie Queen
▷ Mrs. Cleveland's Choice
▷ Boston Tea Party
▷ Prairie Rose

Each block was accompanied by a story written by Nadine Bradley, director of the World-Herald Household Arts Department. The stories related a bit of history behind the block, as well as notes on life at the time the block was originally published.

The Prairie Queen block, the ninth in this series, was published April 11, 1937. The story began, "The small space in the covered wagons made it impossible for the early settlers of the Middle West to take many of their possession with them … But no matter how crowded was the wagon, there was always room to tuck in some of the quilts …" Ms. Bradley continued that as families joined the wagon trains, there was a mingling of favorite quilt patterns, an exchange of designs, and "a desire to create new designs … designs that would be in keeping with their new home." According to Ms. Bradley, it was during those westward treks that the Prairie Queen quilt block was first designed.

Templates for the triangles and squares were printed along with a diagram of the block. Readers were instructed to add the seam allowance. Two colors, a dark and a light — a plain color and white or a plain color and a figured material — should be used, and the blocks could be joined with or without borders.

Not one for always following instructions, I have chosen four fabrics for my quilt rather than two: a purple on white vintage print for the light; a medium purple and dark purple for the blocks; and a third purple for the binding. I chose purple for the wildflower called Blazing Star or Prairie Gayfeather (Liatris). Its tall purple spires waving in the wind were admired and noted in journals by pioneers on their journey across the prairie. The plant still blooms wild in grasslands and has found a home in urban gardens as well.

QUILT SHOW ENTRY
★
I Intend to Enter THE WORLD-HERALD
QUILT CONTEST AND SHOW June 1 to 6.
NAME Mrs. W.F. Wenke
City Pender, Nebr.
Address 200 Fifth Street
I Plan to Enter the Following Division
World-Herald Series
Clip and Mail to WORLD-HERALD QUILT EDITOR
(This blank is not intended as binding the signer to enter but is
designed to gather information as to how many to prepare for at
the exhibit.)

—Prairie Queen—

PIECED BY DONNA DI NATALE
QUILTED BY DONNA SIMPSON
FINISHED BLOCK SIZE: 12" SQUARE
FINISHED QUILT SIZE: 48" X 48"

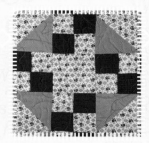

T his quilt can be made of all pieced blocks or pieced blocks set with plain blocks in between, and can be sashed or not. Because the individual blocks are fairly large, 12", and form an interesting pattern when placed next to each other, I chose to not use blank blocks or sashing. The original pattern did not include a border; many of the quilts from this era didn't, so I bound my quilt in purple to give it a finished edge.

Fabric and Supplies

- ▷ 1 5/8 yards light print
- ▷ 3/4 yards medium solid
- ▷ 3/4 yards dark solid
- ▷ 1/2 yard medium dark solid for binding
- ▷ 3 yards backing

Cutting

From light print, cut:

- ▷ 20 − 4 1/2" squares
- ▷ 32 − 4 7/8" squares
- ▷ 8 − 2 1/2" x WOF strips

From medium solid, cut:

- ▷ 32 − 4 7/8" squares

From dark solid, cut:

- ▷ 8 − 2 1/2" x WOF strips

From medium dark solid, cut:

- ▷ 5 − 2 1/2" x WOF strips

Half-Square Triangles

Place one light print 4 7/8" square on top of one medium solid 4 7/8" square, right sides facing. Draw a diagonal line from one corner to the opposite corner. Sew 1/4" on each side of the line. Cut on the drawn line. Press seam toward dark fabric. Make 80 medium/light squares.

Four-Patch Squares

Sew a dark solid 2 1/2" strip and a light print 2 1/2" strip together lengthwise, right sides facing. Press seam toward dark fabric. Make 8 dark solid/light print strip sets.

Cut strip sets into 2 1/2" sections. You will need 128 sections.

Sew two dark solid/light sections together as shown to form a four-patch. Make 64 four-patch blocks.

Assembly

Referring to the block diagram, sew the squares into rows first, and then sew the rows together to make the block. Pay special attention to the placement of each piece in order to achieve the overall pattern.

Referring to the assembly diagram, sew the blocks together in rows of 4. Make 4 rows.

Sew the rows together. Pay special attention to the arrangement of the blocks so that the light print half-square triangle points face inward around the edge.

Quilt, bind and enjoy.

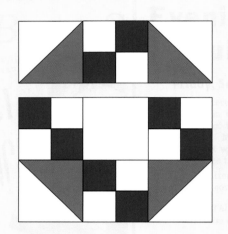

—1938—

Happy days were here again, at least according to the campaign song of Franklin D. Roosevelt, elected to a second term as President in 1938. But articles regarding the World-Herald quilt contest were fewer than in previous years as news stories of the escalating wars in Europe, Asia and Russia filled the pages. Quilt owners were still excited to enter their quilts, and the public looked forward to the free exhibit. The show was co-sponsored by the Orchard & Wilhelm store.

No book on 1930s quilts would be complete without a Grandmother's Flower Garden quilt. How many of you had a grandma or great-grandma who made this iconic 30s quilt pattern? Virtually all of these quilts were hand pieced and hand quilted; many of them were pieced using paper templates, also called English paper piecing. But when searching for quilts, I believe I find more unfinished quilt tops in this pattern than any other. Why? The pattern always has an irregular edge, so that completing the quilt often presents more of a challenge than quilters felt they were up to.

The Petite Grandmother's Flower Garden included here is small, and it is appliquéd to the background fabric, eliminating the need to bind all of those little, irregular shapes. It is made using the English paper piecing method. I find this form of piecing relaxing. It is portable — no sewing machine required. It is perfect for stitching on an airplane or on layovers in airports or waiting almost anywhere. I do most of my English paper piecing while watching television. You can use a machine to join the hexes, but there is so much joy and satisfaction in making something by hand.

Grandmother's Petite —Flower Garden—

MADE BY DONNA DI NATALE
HAND QUILTED BY DONNA DI NATALE
FINISHED SIZE: 23 ½" X 29 ½"

This quilt uses a ¾" paper template (measurement of one side) for the quilt and ½" paper templates for the corner embellishments. Many of the full size quilts from the 30s used a 1 ½" template, but the smaller one looks better on small quilts. Templates can be purchased in various sizes and materials, or you can make your own. Whatever size you use, cut your fabric pieces ½" – ¾" larger than the template.

The flower block in Grandmother's Flower Garden can have as many rows as you want. They can all be the same or each one can be different. It is so much fun to fussy cut your units to create individual flowers, or use stripes to create a kaleidoscope effect.

Something that often baffles people about using hexes is the edge – finishing the irregular edge can be a challenge. This pattern takes care of that problem by using appliqué. The garden is appliquéd to the border. You may think this method wastes fabric but it doesn't. Just use the cut-away piece in your next quilt.

Fabric and Supplies

- Each ¾" hexagon requires a piece of fabric about 1 ½" square. The fabric requirements given for the hexes are broken down into 1 ½" units rather than yardage. The corner embellishment hexes are ½" and use small scraps that are at least 1" square.
- Garden hexes (at least 1 ½" square):
  - Flower centers: 16
  - Flower petals: 96 (6 per flower; 16 flowers)
  - Path: 189
  - Butterflies in path: 12 (or add 12 hexes to the path)
- ½" hexes in corners (at least 1" square): 4 yellow; 8 floral
- Borders (background): ⅔ yard
- Backing: ⅔ yard
- Binding: ¼ yard

- Heavy paper for templates – or purchase precut templates*
- Fabric glue stick (optional)
- Hand sewing needle
- Basting thread (any color)
- Sewing thread in a neutral color

*I highly recommend purchasing pre-cut paper templates. They are inexpensive and save oodles of time.

It's Hexie Time

There are several ways to make the fabric hexagons. This is my favorite way. If you have a different preferred method, use it.

Fabric Scraps or Pieces

The fabric pieces do not need to be exactly square or the exact size – as long as they are at least the size of the template plus ½".

Center and pin or glue baste a paper shape to the reverse side of one of your fabric pieces (see Figure 1).

Pin or glue the paper and fabric in the middle of the hexagon.

Figure 1

Put a knot in your basting thread and start and stop on the right side of the fabric. Carefully fold the edges of the fabric around the paper shape, one side at a time, basting at the folds as you go (see Figures 2 and 3). Keep the folded edges smooth and the corners crisp.

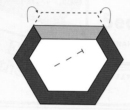

Figure 2

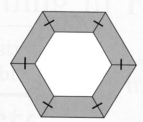

Figure 3

After you baste the last fold, finish the thread on the right side, leaving about an inch of thread. Do not put a knot at the end — you'll just have to cut through it later. Make 16 flower centers, 96 flower petals (6 per flower), 189 stepping stones and 12 butterflies.

Assembling The Gardens

Begin with the center unit. With the paper still inside and right sides together, whip stitch the center to one of the flower units along one edge (see Figure 4). Stay as close to the edge as possible (within a couple of threads), and make sure you don't sew through the paper.

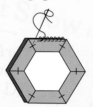

Figure 4

When you get to the end of one side, don't cut the thread. Open the two pieces out.

Place the next flower unit on the center unit, right sides together, and whipstitch the two together, starting where you left off with the first unit (see Figure 5).

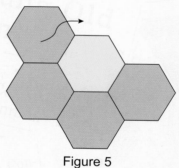

Figure 5

Continue adding pieces around the center unit, until you have a flower unit attached to each side of the center unit (see Figure 6).

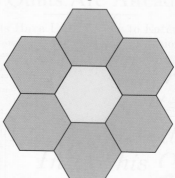

Figure 6

The Garden Paths

You are now ready to attach the stepping stones for the garden path using the same steps. Build your garden row by row or in circles. Once you connect a few, you'll see the garden take shape and figure out how you want your garden to grow. Refer to the photo on page 75, and continue adding garden paths until your garden is complete. Be sure to include the butterflies if you wish.

With the paper templates still in place, take the top to your ironing station. Press the top on both the front and back. I spray mine with Best Press to make sure those hexes really keep their shape. Whatever you do, do not skip this step. Pressing is what keeps the edges of those hexes crisply turned under after you remove the templates.

Removing The Templates

It is time to stitch your garden to the background. But first you need to remove the paper templates. Snip those knots that you left on top of the hexes and pull out the basting stitches. A pair of tweezers is good for pulling out threads. Remove the templates from all the hexes EXCEPT those around the outer edge.

Appliqué

Square and trim the background fabric to 24" x 30" and lay it out on a flat surface, such as a table. Using painter's tape or other repositionable tape, tape the fabric to the table right side up. Starting at the center, smooth the fabric out to the edge and tape it. Go back to the center and smooth to the opposite side. Put another piece of tape there. Repeat on all four sides and the corners, making sure the fabric is flat and smooth.

Center your garden quilt top on the background fabric. Starting at the center and working out, pin the top to the background. Pin every 2" or so — placing a pin in the center of each flower and in between the flowers is perfect.

Now it's time to remove the remaining paper templates. Pin each hexagon to the background as you remove the paper. Be careful to keep the top smooth and flat.

Time to sew the top to the background. Stitch the top to the background either by hand or machine. I appliquéd mine by hand, but use your preferred method.

Turn the top over to the reverse side. See those stitches that attach the garden to the background? Use those stitches as your guide and cut away the background fabric leaving about ½" to ¾" of fabric inside the stitch line. Be careful not to cut into the quilt top. You can just cut away a rectangle; you don't need to follow the jagged edge.

Trim the border to 2 ½" or an equal width on all four sides.

Corner Embellishments

Using the ½" hexagon template, make 4 yellow hexes and 8 floral hexagons in different prints. Sew 3 hexagons together as shown in the photograph. Starch and press.

Position and pin a 3-piece set on each corner. Beginning at one end, appliqué the outer edge of the hexagons. Leave one inside edge of each of the hexagons free.

Remove the basting stitches. Pull out the paper templates, being careful not to stretch the loose edges of the fabric. Use your needle to turn the edge back to the pressed line and continue to appliqué the hexagons in place.

Finishing

It's easy to say quilt and bind and let it go, but if you've made your quilt all by hand so far, why not finish it by hand.

The traditional method for quilting a Grandmother's Flower Garden quilt is to shadow quilt about ¼" from the edge inside each hexagon. You can do this on every hexagon or just some of them. I quilted each center and then around the outer edge of the flower petals. I also quilted the butterflies in the paths and all around the edge of the top, but I did not quilt the paths.

Attach the binding and enjoy!

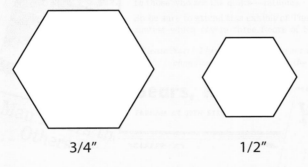

3/4"   1/2"

—1939—

*I*n 1939, the quilt contest and exhibit returned to the original host location – the Brandeis store. Interest seemed to be waning, or perhaps world news was overtaking local interest. Instead of the large 2-column stories of the past, a few of which appeared on the paper's front page, some of the quilt contest announcements were reduced to 1-inch at the bottom of Page 8.

My impression, although not confirmed, is that there was a new editor responsible for the home arts section of the newspaper. Quilt patterns continued to be advertised for sale from the Needle Arts Division, still priced at 10 cents for most patterns, with cute animal and floral appliqué patterns predominating. However, free, full-sized patterns were seldom printed in the paper.

Entries in the contest were slow to come in and the total number entered was never mentioned, nor was there any announcement of attendance at the exhibit. This was unusual, as the "numbers" had always been touted in the past.

The Antique Quilts division was a popular category every year of the contest. Families entered cherished heirlooms brought to America by early immigrants or made by pioneers who settled the new country. Bed covers made from homespun flax or wool woven into fabric were proudly entered for exhibition and competition.

For the first time, a definition of antique was given – "more than 50 years old." Oh gosh, that makes me an antique!

Among the antique quilts there were surely many basket quilts — baskets have always been a popular theme, pieced or appliquéd, or a combination of both, and simple baskets or complex baskets filled with fruit or flowers. This charming little doll quilt was discovered in an antique shop in North Platte, Nebraska. The fabrics date it to around 1880-1900. Just barely an antique in 1939, but truly an antique today.

Antique Basket Doll Quilt

FINISHED QUILT SIZE: 18 ½" SQUARE
FINISHED BLOCK SIZE: 4" SQUARE

A number of doll quilts were created from blocks left over from a larger quilt project, as this one appears to be. How do I know this? The odd "setting triangles" is one way. Some appear to be partial blocks and they are all different sizes. I tried to replicate this quilt and found it impossible to do without making a larger quilt and oddly cutting it down.

If you wish to truly recreate this antique doll quilt, make a few extra blocks to cut and use for setting triangles. Otherwise, follow the instructions for a nice little antique basket quilt. This is an excellent project for using some of the beautiful post-Civil War reproduction fabrics.

Note: If this quilt looks familiar to you, it could be because it was used in the 1978 American Quilt commemorative postage stamps. The stamp was designed by Christopher Pullman, a graphic artist from Boston, and a quilt enthusiast.

Fabric and Supplies

- ▷ 1 − 8" square for each basket (8 total)
- ▷ 1 − 6" square of background for each block (8 total)
- ▷ ¼ yard cheddar solid for sashing
- ▷ Fat quarter light print for setting triangles
- ▷ ²/₃ yard pink print for backing and binding

Cutting

From Each basket fabric, cut:

- ▷ 1 − 3 ⁷/₈" square; cut once diagonally (you will use one triangle per basket)
- ▷ 1 − 1 ⁷/₈" square
- ▷ 1 − 1 ½" x 5" strip for handle

For Each background fabric, cut:

- ▷ 1 − 3 ⁷/₈" square; cut once diagonally (you will use one triangle per basket)
- ▷ 1 − 1 ⁷/₈" square
- ▷ 1 - 1 ½" square
- ▷ 2 - 1 ½" x 2 ½" rectangles

From the cheddar solid, cut:

- ▷ 2 − 2" x WOF strips; subcut into 11 − 2 ½" x 4 ½" strips for block sashing
- ▷ 2 − 2" x WOF strips for row sashing

From the light print, cut:

- ▷ 3 − 7" squares; cut twice diagonally for 8 side triangles
- ▷ 1 − 3 ¾" squares; cut once diagonally for corner triangles

From the pink print, cut:

- ▷ 3 − 2 ¼" x WOF strips for binding

Construction

Fold the ½" x 5" handle strip in half lengthwise, wrong sides together. Sew together using a scant ¼" seam. Trim the seam allowance to ⅛". Turn right side out.

Using a bias bar, press the handle so that the seam allowance is in back and does not show on the sides of the strip.

Pin the handle to background triangle approximately ¾" from the outer edge, mitering the corner.

Topstitch the handle to the background. Trim the ends of the handle even with the long edge of the triangle.

Sew the unit created in step 4 to the basket triangle along the long side.

Place the 1 7/8" basket square on top of the 1 7/8" background square, right sides together. Draw a diagonal line across one square. Sew ¼" on both sides of the line. Cut on drawn line. Open and press. You should have two background/basket half-square triangles.

Assemble The Block

Sew a half-square triangle to one 1 ½" x 2 ½" background rectangle with the basket fabric next to the background rectangle.

Sew the other background rectangle to the remaining b/b half-square triangle with the basket fabric next to the rectangle. Sew the 1 ½" background square to the background side of the b/b half-square triangle.

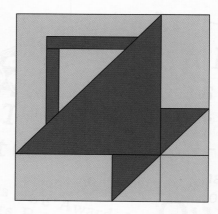

Make 8 blocks total. Refer to the block diagram and stitch the three units together.

Sashing

Refer to the assembly guide and lay out the basket blocks on point. There are two diagonal rows of two blocks and one row with four blocks. Sew 2" x 4 ½" sashing strips between the blocks first.

Add a 2" x 4 ½" sashing strip and side setting triangle to each end of the two rows that have two blocks (the sashing will be trimmed after the quilt top is complete). Stitch a corner setting triangle to each end of the row with four blocks.

Stitch a side setting triangle to each side of the remaining two 4 ½" block sashing strips. These are two corners of the quilt that will be trimmed after completion. Treat these corners as "blocks" when adding the row sashing.

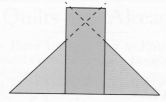

Stitch together the 2 — 2" row sashing strips into one long strip. Subcut the long strip into 2 — 12" strips and 2 — 21" strips. (The sashing strips between the rows are cut longer than needed.)

Stitch the rows and row sashing strips together.
Leave extra sashing on each end to be trimmed.
Carefully trim the sashing to square up the quilt.

Quilt, bind and enjoy!

—1940—

When 1940 rolled around, world events filled the newspapers as the United States drew closer to entering the war. The World-Herald announced another quilt contest, but articles relating to it were smaller and fewer, focusing mainly on the awards. For the first time ever, merchandise certificates rather than specific items were awarded to the winners.

World events did not seem to overshadow interest in the contest. More than 700 quilts were submitted, and viewers numbered into the thousands when the show opened. The value of the quilts was estimated at more than $32,000. This averages about $46 per quilt, or in today's dollars, about $700. Come to think of it, that's about what one might pay for a 1940 quilt on today's market.

The 1940 exhibition included several unique quilts. One was said to be made of more than 42,000 pieces. One was an exact copy, both in color and design, of the original quilt pieced by Abraham Lincoln's mother in the winter before the Civil War president was born. Many quilts expressing patriotism and history were also part of the exhibit.

No mention was ever made of the fact that this would be the last quilt contest, and perhaps no one realized it at the time. Quilt patterns continued to be printed in the paper, and mail order patterns were still popular. But no contest was announced in 1941, and after the United States entered the war, resources were diverted to the war effort. People, and especially women, still made quilts but they also went to work, taking the place of men in factories and industry. Too many lost their husbands in the war, making them the sole supporter of their young family. The 1940s may have changed women's lives forever, but interest in quilts and quilting hasn't changed. The fabrics have changed, designs come and go, and taste in colors and prints will continue to change, but the comfort that quilts provide, whether physical or mental, carries on.

Spinning Pinwheels is adapted from a prize-winning quilt I discovered in a 1974 issue of *McCall's Needlework & Crafts*. A photograph of the quilt was also published in 1975 in *McCall's Book of Quilts*. I loved the design and thought it would make an ideal paper-pieced pattern, and a perfect end to *Prized Quilts*. Enjoy!

—Spinning Pinwheels—

FINISHED SIZE: 70" X 80"
FINISHED BLOCK SIZE: 5"
PIECED BY JANETTE SHELDON
QUILTED BY LINDSAY LAWING

This fabulous scrappy quilt was a prize winner in 1930 at the Illinois State Fair. I know that's a ways from Nebraska, but not all that far, and entries came from all over the country.

It could have been entered in any one of the World-Herald contests. The original pattern was a regular pieced block. However, making all those points come together perfectly put me more in the mind of paper piecing. When I mentioned this to my friend Janette, she immediately jumped in and volunteered to piece the top. You see, Janette is a paper piecing junky. She has made some stunning paper-pieced quilts, so I knew she was the perfect person to test the pattern and make the top.

Janette used Moda's Bella Solids in Yellow (9900 24) to mimic the original fabric, and Lindsay used a similar shade of thread for the quilting. It turned out gorgeous!

Fabric and Supplies

- ▷ Scraps of various prints for pinwheels
- ▷ 5 ½ yards white (or solid scraps) for pinwheels and border #2
- ▷ 2 ½ yards yellow for borders, blocks and binding
- ▷ 5 yards for backing

Cutting

Scrap Pieces

Templates for the pinwheel pieces are provided for those who want to piece this quilt and for those paper-piecers who like to precut their pieces. Please note that the templates include a **½" seam allowance** rather than the usual ¼". This gives plenty of wiggle room for paper piecing.

Just be sure that your pieces fill the space plus seam allowance, and follow the fabric labels on the block layout guide. And be sure to use a few scraps of the border fabric here and there where indicated. Placement of the white pieces relative to the prints and solid is what makes this quilt pop.

From white, cut:

- ▷ 7 – 2 ½" x WOF strips for border #2

From yellow, cut:

- ▷ 6 – 3 ½" x WOF strips for border #1
- ▷ 7 – 5 ½" x WOF strips for border #3
- ▷ 7 – 2 ¼" x WOF strips for binding

Construction

Photocopy the block patterns on page 89 onto your favorite paper-piecing paper. You will need 120 copies each of A and B. I like to make a few extra copies just in case.

Note: Before copying I recommend marking which pieces are always going to be white — A1, B1, A3 and B3.

Cut out each pattern so that you are working with one-half block at a time.

Piece the half blocks starting with piece 1, then 2, 3 and 4. Trim the seam allowances as you sew. Be sure to use a different print or solid for the A2 and A4 and for B2 and B4. This is critical to the overall design. Remember, with paper piecing we're working with the reverse side of the block.

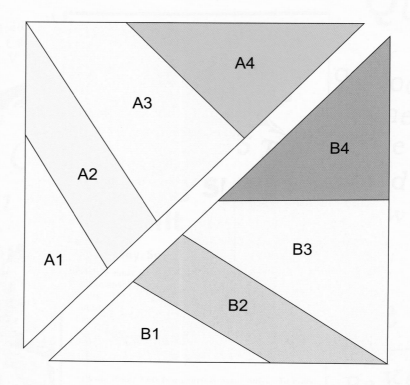

Sew the two half blocks together. As you finish each block, move it to your design wall or a flat surface so you can see the pattern as it develops. This will guide you in arranging the solid and print fabrics in a pleasing design.

When you have all 120 blocks made, sew them together in rows of 10 blocks. Make 12 rows.

Sew the rows together.

It is at this point that I remove the paper pieces. First I stitch about ⅛" from the edge, all the way around the top. Then I remove the papers.

Some of you may want to leave the paper in place until the first border is attached. This is entirely up to you. Just be careful to not stretch or tear the seams as you remove the papers.

Borders

Border #1
Sew the 3 ½" yellow strips together. Measure the quilt from top to bottom. (Janette's measured 60 ½".) Cut two strips to this length and sew to the sides of the quilt. Measure the quilt from side to side (56 ½"). Cut two strips to this length and stitch to the top and bottom.

Border #2
Sew the 2 ½" white strips together. Measure the quilt from top to bottom (66 ½"). Cut two strips to this length and sew to the sides of the quilt. Measure the quilt from side to side (60 ½"). Cut two strips to this length and stitch to the top and bottom.

Border #3
Sew the 5 ½" yellow strips together. Measure the quilt from top to bottom (70 ½"). Cut two strips to this length and sew to the sides of the quilt. Measure the quilt from side to side (70 ½"). Cut two strips to this length and stitch to the top and bottom.

Quilt, bind and enjoy your prized quilt.

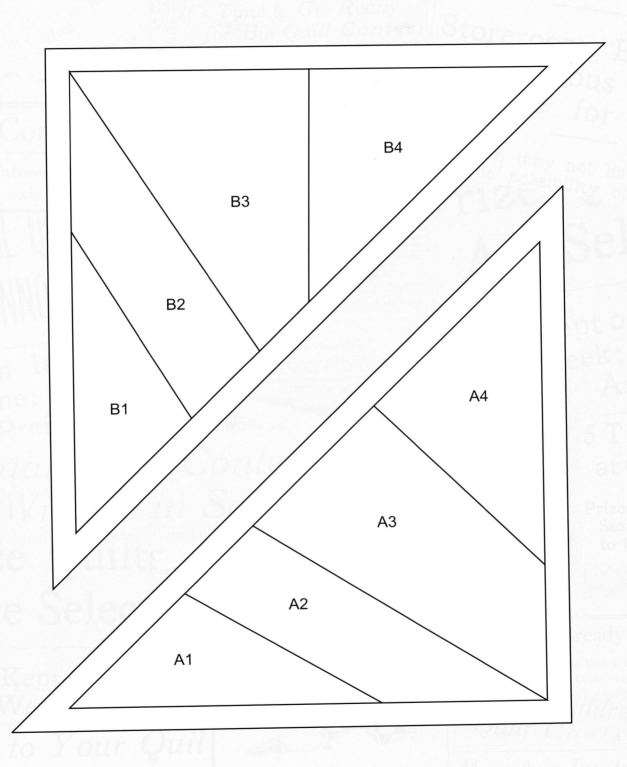

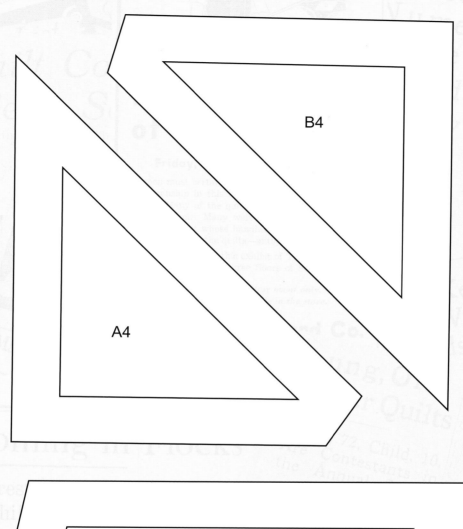

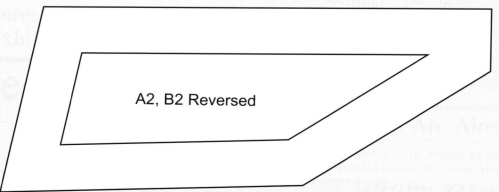

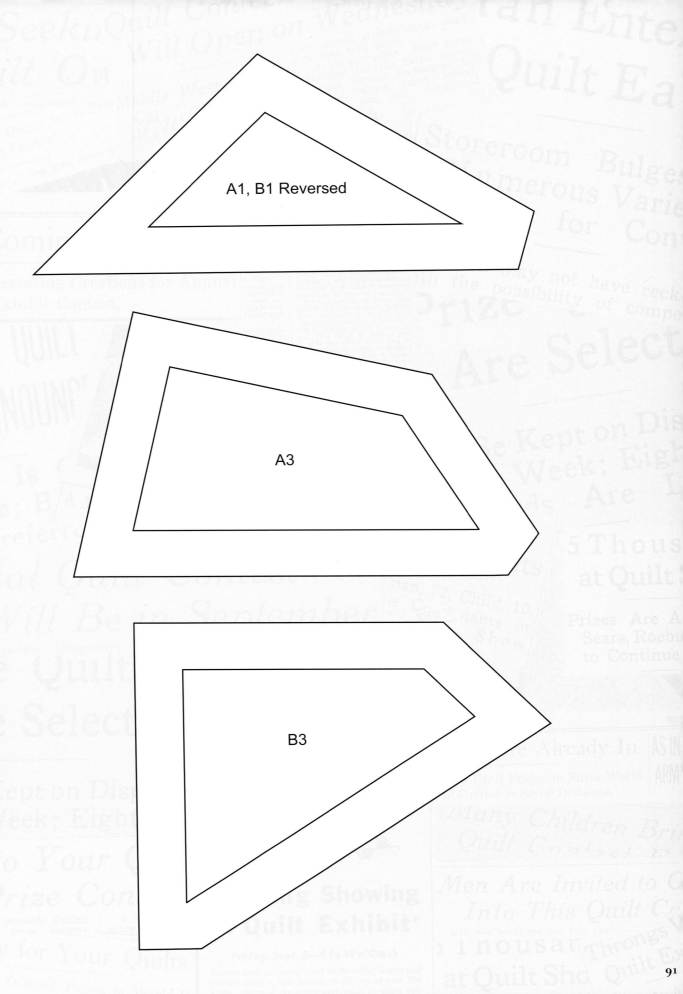

A1, B1 Reversed

A3

B3

More Books from Kansas City Star Quilts

Our Latest Titles

A Basketful of Taupe by Kylie Irvine

A Flock of Feathered Stars: Paper Pieced for Perfection by Carolyn McCormick

A Russian Journey in Quilts: The Story of Nicholas and Nina Filatoff by Tricia Lynn Maloney

Butterfly Fields: A Scrap Quilter's Journey by Carolyn Nixon and Betsey Langford

Colonial Revival Quilts by American Quilt Study Group

Cozy Quilts: A Charming Blend of Wool Appliqué and Cotton Patchwork by Tara Lynn Darr

Farm-Fresh Quilts: Simple Projects Inspired by the Simple Life by Kim Gaddy

Freedom Gone: Embroidered Quilts of Slave Life in the Civil War by Lolita Newman

Fresh from the Prairies: 12 Quilts that Capture the Spirit of the West by Prairie Quilt Mercantile (Lavaigne and Sharon Smith)

It's A Circus: A Parade of Colorful Quilts and More by Amy McClellan

Kindred Spirits: Celebrating Pieces of the Past by Jill Shaulis and Vicki Olsen

Lizzie's Legacy: More Quilts from a Pioneer Woman's Journal by Betsy Chutchian

My Name is Lidya: Inspirations from a Schoolgirl's Sampler by Stacy Nash (a Star Stitch cross stitch book)

Portrait of a Lady by Christina McCourt

Revival! A Study of Early 20th Century Colonia Revival Quilts by the American Quilt Study Group

Sonoran Borders: Threads of Friendship by Vickie Jennett (a Star Stitch cross stitch book)

Tending the Garden: A Blooming Bouquet of Quilts by Barb Adams and Alma Allen of Blackbird Designs

Traditional and Historical Quilts

A Bag of Scraps: Quilts and the Garment District by Edie McGinnis

Across the Wide Missouri: A Quilt Reflecting Life on the Frontier by Edie McGinnis and Jan Patek

Anna's Quilt: A Classic Design for Modern Quilters by Donna di Natale

A Path to the Civil War: Aurelia's Journey Quilt by Sarah Maxwell & Delores Smith

Away from Home: Quilts Inspired by the Lowell Factory Girls by Nancy Rink

A Year of Cozy Comforts: Quilts and Projects for Every Season by Dawn Heese

Border Garden: Kansas Troubles Favorite Projects for Your Home by Lynne Hagmeier

Contemporary to Whimsical Quilts

A Baker's Dozen: 13 Kitchen Quilts by Sandy Klop of American Jane

Adventures with Leaders and Enders: Make More Quilts in Less Time! by Bonnie Hunter

American Summer: Seaside-Inspired Rugs & Quilts by Polly Minick

A Second Helping of Desserts: More Sweet Quilts Using Pre-cut Fabric by Edie McGinnis

Backyard Blooms: A Month by Month Garden Sampler by Barbara Jones

Cabin Fever by Whimsicals

Cottage Charm: Cozy Quilts and Cross Stitch Projects by Dawn Heese

Cradle to Cradle by Barbara Jones of Quilt Soup

Flower Dance: Beautiful Applique Using No-Fail Techniques by Hallye Bone

Fruitful Hands by Jacquelynne Steves

Geese in the Rose Garden by Dawn Heese

Graceful Rhapsody: A Quilted Paisley Block-of-the-Month by Denise Sheehan

Greetings from Tucsadelphia: Travel-Inspired Projects from Lizzie B Cre8ive by Liz & Beth Hawkins

Happy Birthday, Kansas by Linda Frost

Just Desserts: Quick Quilts Using Pre-cut Fabrics by Edie McGinnis

Not Your Grandmother's Quilt: An Applique Twist on Traditional Pieced Blocks by Sheri M. Howard

Picnic Park by Barbara Jones of QuiltSoup

Pieced Hexies: A New Tradition in English Paper Piecing by Mickey Depre

Quilt Retro: 11 Designs to Make Your Own by Jenifer Dick

Reminiscing: A Whimsicals Collection by Terri Degenkolb

Scraps and Shirttails: Reuse, Re-purpose and Recycle! The Art of Green Quilting by Bonnie Hunter

Scraps and Shirttails II: Continuing the Art of Quilting Green by Bonnie Hunter

Some Kind of Wonderful by Anni Downs

Stitched Together: Fresh Projects and Ideas for Group Quilting by Jill Finley

Story Time: Picture Quilts to Stir a Child's Imagination by Kim Gaddy

String Fling: Scrappy, Happy and Loving It! by Bonnie Hunter

Taupe Inspirations: Modern Quilts Inspired by Japanese Taupes by Kylie Irvine

Primitive and Folk Art Quilts

A Bird in Hand: Folk Art Projects Inspired by Our Feathered Friends by Renee Plains

A Bountiful Life: An Adaptation of the Bird of Paradise Quilt Top in the American Folk Art Museum by Karen Mowery

A Day at Sunny Brook: Primitive Projects to Recall Home Life in the 1800s by Maggie Bonanomi

A Little Porch Time: Quilts with a Touch of Southern Hospitality by Lynda Hall

A Stitcher's Journey by Barb Adams and Alma Allen of Blackbird Designs

Birds of a Feather by Barb Adams and Alma Allen of Blackbird Designs

Book of Days by Maggie Bonanomi

Buttonwood Farm: 19 New Primitive Projects by Maggie Bonanomi

Comfort Zone: More Primitive Projects for You and Your Home by Maggie Bonanomi

Country Inn by Barb Adams and Alma Allen of Blackbird Designs

Home Sweet Home by Barb Adams and Alma Allen of Blackbird Designs

Nature's Offerings: Primitive Projects Inspired by the Four Seasons by Maggie Bonanomi

With These Hands: 19th Century-Inspired Primitive Projects for Your Home by Maggie Bonanomi

You're Invited! Quilts and Homes to Inspire by Barb Adams and Alma Allen of Blackbird Designs

Meet the Author

Donna is a third-generation quilter. Her mother, grandmother and aunt all were quilters. Some quilted out of necessity, others for pure pleasure. When she was 5 years old, she was given an embroidery kit as a birthday gift. Her mother taught her how to embroider the designs on the pre-stamped fabric and then taught her how to turn those small pieces into a quilt for her doll, using a little hand-turned Singer sewing machine. That little quilt disappeared long ago, but her love of quilts and quilting is still strong.

Donna is also a quilt collector. Her collection began when she discovered the quilts her mother had stored away in the attic — quilts that her mother, aunt and grandmother had made. The fabrics in those quilts from the 1930s-50s told so many stories.

When Donna saw quilts in antique shops, they would call out to be taken home and loved. They spoke of the women who had lovingly toiled to make these beautiful works of art. She simply could not leave them stacked on shelves or thrown in the corner of a booth, and thus her pile of quilts grew. Soon her collection turned into a passion; estate sales, garage sales, and friends all became sources of quilts needing a loving home.

Today her passion is also her livelihood. When she's not quilting she's editing books for Kansas City Star Quilts, an occupation that has given her the opportunity to meet and work with talented quilters from around the world. She and her husband love to travel, and Donna enjoys seeking out unusual fabrics, patterns and more quilts wherever they go.